MAKING REGIONAL INTEGRATION WORK

COMPANY PERSPECTIVES ON NON-TARIFF MEASURES IN ARAB STATES

Geneva 2015

ABSTRACT FOR TRADE INFORMATION SERVICES

ID= 43162   2015   C-00 000 MAK

International Trade Centre (ITC)
Making regional integration work – Company perspectives on non-tariff measures in Arab States
Geneva: ITC, 2015. XIV, 56 pages.

This report forms part of an ITC series of developing-country survey projects on non-tariff measures (NTMs), for which 25 reports have been issued to date. This is the first report to look at country surveys in a regional context. It analyses four business surveys conducted by ITC in Egypt, Morocco, the State of Palestine and Tunisia, giving governments a glimpse into what businesses perceive as their main challenges to trade, within and beyond the region, and offers insights into the major bottlenecks hampering international and regional trade in the Arab region, by sharing the perspectives of exporters and importers in the region. The surveys focus on NTMs that governments impose; procedures that make compliance difficult; and inefficiencies in the trade-related business environment.

Descriptors: **Arab States, Non-Tariff Measures, Regional Integration, Intraregional Trade, Market Surveys.**

For further information on this publication, contact Ursula Hermelink (ntm@intracen.org).

English

The International Trade Centre (ITC) is the joint agency of the World Trade Organization and the United Nations.

ITC, Palais des Nations, 1211 Geneva 10, Switzerland (www.intracen.org)

The designations employed do not imply the expression of any opinion on the part of the International Trade Centre concerning the legal status of any country, territory, city or area or of its authorities, or concerning the delimitation of its frontiers or boundaries.

Digital image(s) on the cover: © Shutterstock.com

Doc. No. P259.E/DMD/MAR/15-X

ISBN: 978-92-9137-426-7
United Nations Sales No. E.15.III.T.5

FOREWORD

In today's global trade landscape, deeper regional integration is an important policy choice that governments can make to ensure the creation of markets for their small and medium-sized enterprises (SMEs). The Arab region has made integration and better connection of its markets a priority, but the figures show that compared with other regions, intra-Arab trade remains low, despite a number of existing regional trade agreements.

This publication on intra-Arab trade seeks to provide greater information and transparency on the integration story in the region and to do this through the lens of the SMEs. It brings a new perspective to some of the underlying economic forces at work, and suggests that the move to enhanced integration is on an upward trajectory. By boosting the trade capacity of regional SMEs, and their opportunities to access markets, growth and job creation will follow. But there is a need to better identify and address the existing constraints they face.

ITC's enterprise-level analysis of four economies in the region provides insight into the practical day-to-day challenges these enterprises face. Addressing non-tariff measures (NTMs), and ensuring regional market regulation compliance, are just two of the areas that are examined in the publication.

The analysis, however, suggests that many of these barriers can be addressed locally, nationally and regionally. The key message is that market access begins at home, and that there is greater scope for governments to streamline processes, harmonize regulations in the region, and work with exporters to provide consistent, transparent and timely information.

The good news is that Arab leaders and institutions recognize the untapped opportunity for business and investment. They are taking action through regional dialogue, transparency and efficiency initiatives, and through ensuring that enabling policies are in place to ease the cost and time of doing business and of trading in the region.

This publication is the latest in ITC's series of publications that capture company perspectives on NTMs. Over the past five years, ITC has documented business experiences through its NTM Surveys and has interviewed over 15,000 exporters and importers in 30 developing countries.

We hope that this publication will serve as a foundation to facilitate trade, particularly for the SMEs in the region. ITC remains committed to supporting the Arab region in achieving regional trade impact for good.

Arancha González
ITC Executive Director

ACKNOWLEDGEMENTS

This publication was written by Ursula Hermelink and Mathieu Loridan based on the data from the International Trade Centre (ITC) business surveys on non-tariff measures (NTMs) in Egypt, Morocco, the State of Palestine and Tunisia.

The authors thank Mondher Mimouni for his guidance in the analysis, Abdellatif Benzakri for the preparation of statistics and analytical contributions, as well as Khemraj Ramful and Julia Spies for additional inputs. They thank stakeholders and colleagues, particularly Lilia Naas, Abdeslam Azuz, Mena Hassan, Kenza Le Mentec, Saskia Marx, Lionel Fontagné and Helen Lassen, for valuable comments and feedback.

ITC expresses its gratitude to all speakers, discussants and participants in the high-level roundtable on non-tariff measures, held in Tunis, 28–29 April 2014, for contributing concrete proposals and recommendations.

ITC is grateful to the representatives of enterprises and experts who agreed to be interviewed and to share their experiences with NTM-related trade obstacles.

Further thanks are extended to Dianna Rienstra, Erica Meltzer and Natalie Domeisen for editing; Evelyn Seltier and Natalie Domeisen for production management; Kristina Golubic for design; Laurena Arribat for photo research; and Serge Adeagbo and Franco Iacovino for printing.

ITC acknowledges the financial support of the United Kingdom's Department for International Development (DFID) and the Government of Canada to the NTM Surveys in the Arab region, as well as of the United States Agency for International Development (USAID) and the International Islamic Trade Finance Corporation (ITFC) to the Tunis roundtable.

CONTENTS

TABLES

FIGURES

ABBREVIATIONS

COMESA	Common Market for Eastern and Southern Africa
EU	European Union
FTA	Free trade agreement
GAFTA	Greater Arab Free Trade Area
GSP	Generalized System of Preferences
ITC	International Trade Centre
LDC	Least developed country
NTM	Non-tariff measure
OECD	Organisation for Economic Co-operation and Development
RoW	Rest of the world
SME	Small and medium-sized enterprise
SPS	Sanitary and phytosanitary
TBT	Technical barriers to trade
TISI	Trade and investment support institution
WTO	World Trade Organization

EXECUTIVE SUMMARY

Regional integration has been a key to improving business prospects. As transportation and e-connectivity have improved, it has been easier for businesses to reach new markets, and for consumer purchasing power to grow.

Governments have supported these trends with preferential trade agreements within their regions, particularly as the pace of complex multilateral trade negotiations has slowed. All but a few countries have signed preferential trade agreements within their region. As a result, tariffs have often been eliminated or dramatically reduced.

Trade barriers today are often the result of non-tariff measures (NTMs). They go far beyond tariff measures, keeping markets highly fragmented. Those who trade across borders must comply with many technical regulations, product standards and customs procedures. Their compliance challenges cut into the potential for regional trade, spelling lost opportunities for governments and firms, and missed employment opportunities for individuals.

REGIONAL CHALLENGES TO TRADE

Intraregional trade among Arab States is low compared to other regions. Most of this intraregional trade is in basic commodities and agricultural products. Regional trade in high-technology goods is below average.

To diversify and boost trade, especially by small and medium-sized enterprises (SMEs), policymakers need to understand the bottlenecks that keep the Greater Arab Free Trade Area (GAFTA, the regional preferential trade agreement set up in 1997 among members of the League of Arab States) agreement and other regional agreements from reaching their potential.

BUSINESS INSIGHTS

This publication offers insights into those bottlenecks, by sharing the perspectives of exporters and importers in the region. It analyses four business surveys conducted by ITC in Egypt, Morocco, the State of Palestine and Tunisia, giving governments a glimpse into what businesses perceive as their main challenges to trade, within and beyond the region.

The surveys focus on NTMs that governments impose; procedures that make compliance difficult; and inefficiencies in the trade-related business environment. They form part of an ITC series of developing-country survey projects on NTMs, for which 25 reports have been issued to date. This is the first report to look at country surveys in a regional context.

The insights can be used to boost trade within the Arab region, especially by addressing quality requirements, customs procedures and the implementation of trade agreements. The survey findings are also being used to inform sectoral, national and regional measures that reduce the compliance costs of moving goods and services across borders. The regional recommendations in this publication are based on a high-level regional roundtable on NTMs (Tunis, April 2014).

The surveys, conducted at the request of the States concerned, were done in Arabic or French by ITC staff and partner organizations. They drew from a sample frame of 11,662 companies in local business registries and membership lists of business associations and trade support institutions; 1,921 telephone interviews and 855 face-to-face interviews were conducted in all. The surveys help address the following questions: Who is affected by burdensome NTMs, and to what extent? Which NTMs are perceived as burdensome, and why? What procedural

Survey findings at a glance

- NTMs have a significant impact on exporters in Arab States.
- Trade agreements on preferential market access do not insulate against NTM-related problems.
- Arab States are responsible for a disproportionate share of reported cases of burdensome regulations, relative to their importance as an export destination.
- More problematic than NTMs themselves are related procedural obstacles, which increase the cost of compliance.

- Conformity assessment measures and rules of origin are especially challenging.
- The private sector has difficulties in understanding and complying with product quality requirements.
- Inefficient testing and certificate procedures are compounded by insufficient infrastructure.
- Domestic barriers comprise a large share of reported obstacles.

obstacles do exporters/importers encounter, and where do the obstacles occur?

REGIONAL NTM PATTERNS

In the four surveys, 44% of all trading companies (both exporters and importers) reported facing burdensome NTMs – both within and outside the region. A significant share of NTMs emanate from the home country – 24% for agriculture and 21% for manufacturing. This is in line with ITC findings in other countries and regions, which show that many barriers originate at home.

Differences among the four cases are pronounced due to differing trade patterns. In line with its trade structure, Morocco reports far fewer cases involving Arab States than the average, and relatively more cases concerning the European Union (EU). The opposite holds true for Egypt. For the State of Palestine, many cases concern NTMs applied by Israel.

Some 37% of the burdensome NTMs reported by agricultural exporters are applied by regional trading partners, while only 34% of their exports go to the Arab region. For manufacturing, 47% of NTM cases concern Arab States' regulations, compared with only 16% of their exports.

SPS MEASURES AND TBT

Survey respondents perceived sanitary and phytosanitary (SPS) measures and technical barriers to trade (TBTs) as the most challenging NTMs. More than half (54%) of the NTM cases cited fall into this category, which comprises technical regulations and conformity assessment measures. Companies had many more problems in complying with conformity assessment measures of countries within the region than with technical regulations themselves.

Product quality and conformity challenges include:

- Insufficient private-sector capacity to comply with technical regulations;
- Difficult labelling requirements;
- Inefficient testing and certification procedures;
- High certification costs;
- Lack of recognition of certificates and lack of harmonization of standards;
- Lack of transparency of foreign standards and conformity assessment procedures;
- Lengthy product registration and import authorization procedures.

RULES OF ORIGIN

Rules of origin pose a major challenge for exporters in the region. Regional and bilateral agreements have established tariff-free market access in principle. To benefit from tariff preferences, companies must prove the origin of their products. Trade agreements have thus ended up replacing tariffs with non-tariff measures.

This is not necessarily problematic. For example, for trading with the EU, only 6% of reported NTM-related problems concern rules of origin. Rules of origin, however, do appear to be a significant challenge within the region.

Recurrently reported problems include failure to grant preferential treatment, language issues, inefficiency in issuing the certificates of origin, and specific problems related to 'made in Palestine'.

Numerous exporters report that despite compliance with rules of origin under any or all of the agreements governing trade between two Arab States, companies are not granted preferential treatment and are obliged to pay tariffs. The main agreements are GAFTA, the Agadir Agreement and the Common Market for Eastern and Southern Africa (COMESA).

CUSTOMS CLEARANCE AND BORDER CONTROLS

Customs authorities may be the single most important trade facilitation body.

They balance a mandate of revenue collection, product quality and safety control against smooth import and export procedures. Inappropriate infrastructure is a major challenge, including outdated scanners and missing, ill-equipped or expensive storage facilities.

Another challenge is the availability and training of officials. Exporters report limited service hours and staff shortages for inspections and customs clearance. They also report poorly trained inspection personnel, resulting in product damage during inspections.

Procedures change frequently and there is not enough access to customs clearance information and related documents. Bottlenecks and delays occur when companies are unprepared for customs.

Businesses also report a lack of coordination and trust between agencies and countries.

The result: Customs clearance procedures are perceived as lengthy, bureaucratic, disorganized and costly.

OTHER NTM CHALLENGES

Other challenges include quantity control measures (licences, quotas, etc.), charges and taxes, and finance measures (such as regulations on payment terms for imports or on official foreign exchange allocations). Together, these measures represent 25% of challenging NTMs regionally, in contrast to 13% in countries outside the region.

Outside the region, the EU market poses the most challenges for quantity control measures on agricultural products. Problematic pre-shipment inspections (5%) are mainly driven by Israeli inspections of Palestinian exports.

Among export-related measures applied by the home country, businesses are concerned most frequently about export taxes, registration and licensing requirements, and export permits.

A BETTER BUSINESS ENVIRONMENT FACILITATES TRADE

Most NTMs are not in themselves problematic, especially for manufacturing products. However, the related procedures make compliance difficult. For example, an exporter may comply with the tolerance limit for pesticides, yet be unable to prove it because the accredited testing laboratory is too costly or far away.

For intraregional agricultural exports, businesses would not have reported one fourth of the cases if procedures had been smoother, and another third would have been considered less onerous.

For manufacturing, procedural obstacles are even higher, accounting for nearly half of the problems that were reported for NTMs applied by regional trading partners, and nearly two thirds of those applied at home.

The national business environment also makes a difference. Issues include:

- Lack of port security, which exposes goods to theft;
- Poor transport infrastructure;
- Insufficient space on air carriers for merchandise transport, which biases them towards large companies;
- Bribes;
- Lack of computerized processes;
- Lack of access to finance, information and counselling.

This suggests that many obstacles to intraregional trade could be reduced by tackling procedural obstacles and enhancing the business environment – that is, by facilitating trade rather than changing the underlying trade rules.

RECOMMENDATIONS

Below are recommendations to address the regional challenges to trade identified in the NTM surveys.

They incorporate the recommendations of a 2014 regional roundtable on NTMs, involving ministries of trade, standards bodies and customs agencies from 10 Arab States, as well as regional organizations and donors.

TRANSPARENCY IS CROSS-CUTTING

Transparency is a cross-cutting issue, cited frequently by survey respondents.

Recommendations focus on better data collection, information dissemination and capacity-building:

- Publish, update and disseminate official procedures, deadlines, response times and fees for all institutions involved in the export and import process. Use web-based portals, brochures, helpdesks and helplines, and ensure regular opening days.
- Adopt a tracking system with enquiry mechanisms so that companies can follow their requests and ask for an official response when deadlines are not respected.

Key recommendations

- **Market access begins at home**. The upside of home-made problems is that they can be solved more easily than those outside a country's or region's jurisdiction. The survey findings underscore the fact that there is wide scope for action on tackling the *before-the-border* problems confronting businesses with *behind-the-border* measures.

- **Streamline procedures**. Many intraregional trade obstacles could be resolved by streamlining procedures – that is, by facilitating trade rather than by changing trade rules.

- **Make trade agreements work**. The survey findings support the conventional wisdom that having policies, laws and agreements is one thing, but effectively implementing them is another. Making existing agreements work – including GAFTA, mutual recognition agreements, the revised Kyoto Convention and the Trade Facilitation Agreement of the World Trade Organization (WTO) – can help facilitate trade and would eliminate many business concerns about NTMs.

- **Transparency facilitates trade**. Procedures may sometimes be complicated and lengthy for good reasons. There is no good reason for them to be unclear or poorly disseminated. Providing information makes procedures more efficient and lowers costs, by making cross-border business transactions more predictable in terms of time and cost.

- **Upgrade infrastructure for quality standards**. As the Arab world seeks to enhance product quality standards for the benefit of consumers, infrastructure-related problems in intraregional trade will grow if they are not addressed.

- **Train companies on quality, traceability and related documentation**. Raising the capacity of Arab companies to produce high-quality products and to better document production processes and ingredients' origin and composition (traceability) would benefit trade in general, both within and beyond the region.

- Remedy the information gap through a comprehensive regional trade information portal on market access conditions, regulations and related procedures in Arab States.
- Set up a regional network to exchange information and coordinate with national enquiry points.
- Produce regional export guides on labelling and traceability requirements, quality standards and related processes, and customs procedures.
- Increase regional business matchmaking opportunities provided by trade and investment support institutions (TISIs).
- Offer ongoing, in-depth training for the private and public sector on international trade agreements.
- Enhance TISI advisory services to SMEs, particularly in remote areas.
- Hold regular training sessions on product certification and customs clearance procedures.

SIMPLIFY QUALITY REQUIREMENTS AND CONFORMITY ASSESSMENT

Three types of measures stand out as problematic in this area: product certification, testing, and labelling requirements.

- Identify priority sectors and products based on their potential to drive regional integration. Concentrate standard-setting efforts in the conformity assessment infrastructure on priority areas.
- Review regional standardization and conformity assessment strategies to identify gaps. Coordinate regional negotiating positions in the international standard-setting process.
- Draw up an inventory of regional standards. Evaluate them against international standards.
- Increase efforts to harmonize national standards and technical requirements.
- Help national standards bodies and the private sector to participate in regional standard-setting. Step up support to sector-specific trade associations, in line with identified intraregional trade priorities.
- Examine national conformity assessment procedures, including testing, certification and inspection procedures. Draft a regional harmonization roadmap. Map demand for and public and private supply of laboratory testing for priority sectors.
- Assess the business model for laboratories. Designate reference laboratories to address regional testing needs. Upgrade technical infrastructure, support accreditation and improve accessibility from abroad.
- Strengthen key national inspection and certification bodies to comply with international requirements and accreditation criteria.
- Ensure mutual recognition of test results and certification to avoid costly duplication. Review mutual recognition

agreements and memoranda for conformity assessment to identify implementation obstacles, and support countries and institutions in eliminating such obstacles.
- Create sustainable financial mechanisms, particularly for SMEs, to upgrade production processes, traceability and product quality in line with international requirements, and make testing and certification affordable.
- Make training on quality requirements more affordable for smaller enterprises and those in remote areas.
- Harmonize labelling requirements, for example through a standardized 'Arab label' in Arabic, French and English.

Improve the regulatory framework

- Raise awareness and promote effective implementation of good regulatory practices. Assess national legislation on SPS measures; TBTs; and related conformity assessment procedures in the light of WTO agreements.
- Promote national best practices of market surveillance and ensure regional coordination, setting up a coordination mechanism among national regulatory institutions, inspection bodies and TISIs.

ADDRESS TRADE-RELATED MEASURES

Trade policy-related recommendations are difficult to formulate, as their viability depends on the political priority given to regional trade integration.

As a start, countries can look at measures they impose on their own exporters. Trade facilitation can and should happen at home, independent from partner-country commitments. These challenges underscore the importance of transparency and access to trade-related information. Work should focus on procedural obstacles and trade support infrastructure as well as on trade rules and agreements.

Reduce procedural obstacles

- Invest in people to avoid frequent staff turnover and reduce administrative delays.
- Invest in trade support infrastructure, and particularly in electronic document submission and information storage systems, to alleviate administrative burdens.
- Implement fast-track procedures for companies that repeatedly export the same products within a short period of time.
- Institutionalize ongoing public-private dialogue through national trade facilitation committees.
- Strengthen TISI networks and their outreach to small enterprises and remote areas.
- Provide key regional TISIs with access to dedicated platforms, thereby enhancing their capacity to lobby for improving domestic business environments.

- Address wider business environment issues, including SME access to trade finance, trade-related services and transport infrastructure and logistics.

Facilitate implementation of existing agreements

The region lacks effective national and regional mechanisms to monitor implementation of agreements and to resolve implementation issues.

- Create a trade obstacles alert by setting up enquiry points or helpdesks for the private sector to handle complaints about obstacles to intraregional trade.
- Develop capacity to use existing trade agreements.
- Clarify and harmonize rules of origin, and implement the WTO Trade Facilitation Agreement in all countries in the region, WTO Members and non-members alike.

Review regional trade policy

- Evaluate GAFTA measures that limit preferential trade and implement less trade-distorting alternatives.
- Close GAFTA loopholes and build an institutional structure to formulate, implement and better monitor joint policies. Improve regional coordination of trade policies, technical cooperation on harmonizing rules and procedures, and dispute settlement mechanisms. Review the role of the Arab Economic and Social Council and establish GAFTA-specific bodies.

Assist least developed Arab States

- More advanced Arab States could provide technical and financial assistance to develop their neighbours' capacities in the areas of trade rules, customs clearance and trade infrastructure.

STREAMLINE CUSTOMS CLEARANCE AND BORDER CONTROLS

Efficient risk management, paperless customs clearance, and learning from the success stories of other countries are central to rationalizing border formalities.

- Review customs legislation, improve customs infrastructure and streamline customs procedures using information and communication technologies (ICTs).
- Strengthen partnerships and information exchange between the customs authorities in the region and beyond.
- Strengthen human resources at customs authorities and border stations to speed up clearance. Provide customs officials with ongoing training, for example in cooperation with the World Customs Organization or customs authorities from other countries.

- Institute a sweeping cultural change so that customs authorities consider themselves a 'welcome point' and are proud of the role they play in national well-being, security, economic development and regional integration.

REPORT STRUCTURE

Chapter 1 has an introduction to the trade context in the region. It outlines overlapping preferential agreements, the role of tariff preferences and NTMs and other intraregional trade obstacles reported by the surveys.

Chapter 2 has an overview of the survey findings.

Chapters 3–5 summarize obstacles in three main areas: product quality and conformity; rules of origin and other trade-related measures; and customs clearance and border controls. Conclusions are contained in Chapter 6, which also summarizes the recommendations from the Tunis roundtable.

CHAPTER I

REGIONAL OVERVIEW

REGIONAL OVERVIEW

All but a few countries have signed preferential trade agreements within their region. Intraregional trade has not, however, surged everywhere. Obstacles remain that go far beyond conventional tariff measures, keeping markets fragmented. This trend ignores the potential for regional trade, spelling lost opportunities for governments and firms, and missed employment opportunities for individuals.

Identifying major bottlenecks to greater regional integration is a crucial first step towards making regional preferential trade agreements work. This publication examines regional integration among Arab States and aims to inform the ongoing discussion on the potential for stronger regional integration.

It draws on insights from comprehensive surveys of exporters' and importers' perspectives on non-tariff measures (NTMs), carried out in Egypt, Morocco, the State of Palestine and Tunisia under the International Trade Centre (ITC) NTM programme, to identify trade obstacles in the region. Chapters 2–5 served as the background document for a high-level regional roundtable on NTMs, held in Tunis on 28–29 April 2014.

OVERLAPPING PREFERENTIAL AGREEMENTS

Despite ongoing efforts to cut tariffs and to sign and implement preferential agreements, regional trade integration among the members of the League of Arab States is modest compared with other common markets, such as the European Union (EU) and the Association of Southeast Asian Nations (ASEAN).

Arab States have signed numerous trade agreements on preferential market access, many of which overlap (figure 1). The Greater Arab Free Trade Area (GAFTA) comprises all League members except Comoros, Djibouti, Mauritania and Somalia.

Within GAFTA, the six Gulf countries form the Gulf Cooperation Council, while Egypt, Jordan, Morocco and Tunisia are parties to the Agadir Agreement for establishing a Mediterranean free trade area. A number of bilateral agreements between Arab States, most of which were implemented before GAFTA, still exist. Although in principle they are superseded by GAFTA, they may still be used for preferential trade, in particular where rules of origin differ from those stipulated by GAFTA.

TARIFF PREFERENCES HAVE NOT TRANSLATED INTO REGIONAL INTEGRATION

Even though tariffs have been largely eliminated since the mid-1990s as a result of bilateral agreements, regional integration has not caught up. As a result, trade among Arab States remains low compared with other regions. The highest intraregional trade shares involve basic commodities and agricultural products.

By contrast, high-technology goods show below-average intraregional trade shares, but are among those most intensively traded with the EU.

NON-TARIFF MEASURES – PREVENTING TRADE AMONG ARAB STATES?

In the global context of more open markets and lower tariffs, trade obstacles resulting from NTMs have grown in importance. Exporting companies seeking access to foreign markets and companies importing products must comply with a wide range of requirements, including technical regulations, product standards and customs procedures. NTMs vary across products, sectors and countries, and can change quickly. Most of these regulations do not have protectionist objectives, but seek to protect public health, the environment, social or labour conditions. However, compliance is sometimes difficult for firms, particularly small and medium-sized enterprises (SMEs).

SURVEYS POINT TO INTRAREGIONAL TRADE OBSTACLES

This publication presents evidence from business surveys that ITC carries out under its NTM programme. Building on the experience and knowledge of export and import businesses in dealing with NTMs, the survey findings enhance understanding of the perception and impact of NTMs, which by their nature are hard to quantify. The survey findings identify at product, sector and partner-country level the predominant obstacles businesses face when complying with NTMs. They also pinpoint potential bottlenecks to the capabilities and technical capacity

Figure 1: Trade agreements involving Arab States

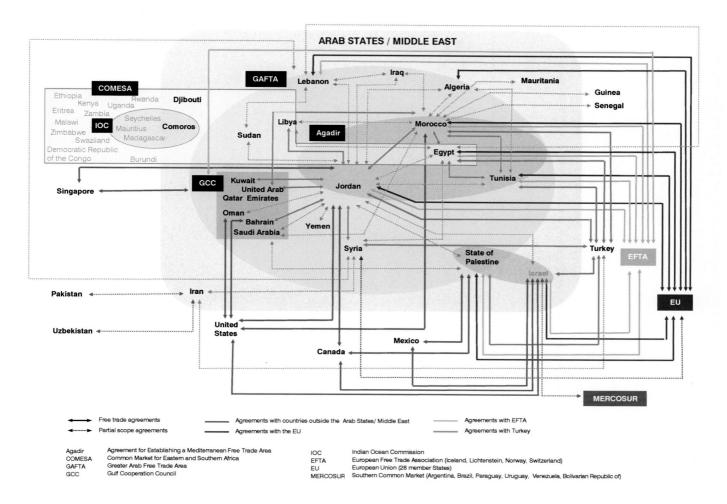

Note: To the best of ITC's knowledge, this figure reflects the situation as of October 2015. Included are implemented agreements concerning trade in goods only. The number and list of products to which preferences are granted varies from country/territory to country/territory. Only agreements with reciprocal preferences are shown. The countries depicted here may be granted preferential tariffs resulting from trade regimes such as the Generalized System of Preferences (GSP), i.e. from countries providing non-reciprocal preferential tariffs to developing and least developed countries.

for complying with regulations and for demonstrating compliance at the national level.

The ITC NTM programme conducted surveys in Egypt, Morocco, the State of Palestine and Tunisia between 2010 and 2012. (Additional surveys in the region are envisaged under the Aid for Trade Initiative for the Arab States, which started in 2015.) While the findings of the four surveys are not representative of the Arab region as a whole, they do provide insights into the obstacles reported by exporters with regard to trade with other Arab States.

Based on these findings, this publication analyses the main NTM-related obstacles to intraregional trade in three key areas:

• Product quality and conformity
• Rules of origin and other trade-related measures
• Customs clearance and border controls.

CHAPTER 2

NTM SURVEY FINDINGS IN ARAB STATES

NTM SURVEY FINDINGS IN ARAB STATES

The ITC NTM Surveys cover Egypt, Morocco, the State of Palestine and Tunisia. The findings reflect the private sector's perspective on NTM-related trade obstacles and provide a springboard to discuss concrete actions that reduce trade costs.

BACKGROUND AND METHODOLOGY

The four surveys covered here (table 1) are part of a series that have been conducted in over 25 countries under the ITC programme on NTMs, which is financed primarily by the United Kingdom Department for International Development (DFID).[1] The survey process and analysis of its findings are based on a global methodology[2] with adjustments made for country specificities.

- The survey material, including the questionnaires and the NTM classification, was translated into Arabic. Interviews were conducted in Arabic or French.

- In Egypt, the survey was implemented a few months after the January 2011 revolution. As companies were asked about the previous 12 months of their export-import activities, the findings cover the period both before and after the change of government. The types of findings

obtained for Egypt are not significantly different from those in other countries, which suggests that the political instability in the country had a limited impact on the survey.

- In Morocco, the survey was carried out in the framework of the ITC Enhancing Arab Capacity for Trade Programme (EnAct). The methodology was the same as in other countries.

- In the State of Palestine, the survey was implemented by PalTrade, the national trade promotion organization (TPO), as part of a Canadian-funded project (Export Development for Palestinian Business Project in the West Bank). In the context of this project, it was decided to focus only on export activities. ITC NTM Surveys in other countries cover both the export and the import perspectives. The questionnaire had an additional section with questions on PalTrade membership and services, which served as a needs assessment for other project activities. The global methodology was amended for the interviews. In contrast to the two-stage process in other countries, consisting of telephone interviews followed by face-to-face interviews, all interviews were held face-to-face. Nearly the entire population of actively exporting enterprises was contacted (with 239 out of 513 companies willing to answer the NTM-related questions), and the sample size thus exceeds the requirements for representativeness.

Table 1: NTM Surveys in Morocco, Egypt, State of Palestine and Tunisia

	Organization that implemented the survey	Interview period	Total number of companies in the sample frame	Number of interviews	
				Telephone interviews	Face-to-face
Morocco	LMS-CSA Marketing & Sondages	April 2010–February 2011	3,264	794	256
Egypt	The International Company for Export Development – ExpoFront	May–November 2011	3,017	869	189
State of Palestine	PalTrade	December 2011–March 2012	513	n.a.	239
Tunisia	Carthage University, Tunis	July–August 2011 and July–October 2012	4,868	258	171

---

1   More information about the ITC programme on NTMs is available from www.intracen.org/ntm.

2   For more information on the methodology underlying the surveys and the analysis of their findings, see ITC (2015), The invisible barriers to trade – How businesses perceive non-tariff measures, available from www.intracen.org/publications/ntm (accessed 15 September 2015).

Figure 2: Share of the surveyed economies in total Arab States' exports

Agricultural

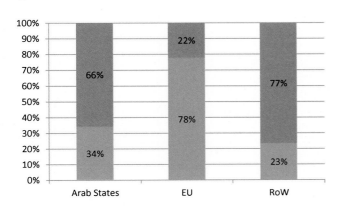

Manufacturing

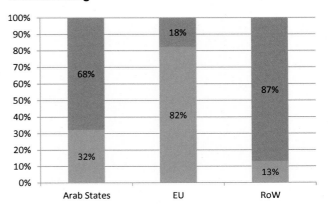

■ Egypt, Morocco, State of Palestine and Tunisia   ■ Other Arab States

Source: ITC calculations based on ITC Trade Map data, 2013.

The four surveyed economies' exports of agricultural products to the EU represent 78% of all Arab States' exports of agricultural products to the EU. They also account for 32% of manufacturing exports within the Arab region.

Notes: Total exports exclude minerals and arms.

- In Tunisia, company interviews were divided into two different time periods for logistical and political reasons. Companies exporting agricultural products were interviewed in 2011, while those trading manufacturing products were surveyed in 2012. Despite the time lag, the findings do not differ significantly from those in countries where the interviews were conducted within a single period.

The surveys allow for an analysis of the private-sector perspective on NTM-related trade obstacles, with a view to identifying concrete actions that will enable countries to achieve greater efficiency in the export process and to reduce trade costs. The analysis provides insight into the following questions:

- **Who is affected by burdensome NTMs, and to what extent?**
  Sectors, products, types of companies (women/men-owned, size, region), partner countries, and type of trade flow (export/import).

- **Why are NTMs perceived as burdensome?**
  Strict regulations, procedural obstacles or both.

- **Which NTMs are perceived as burdensome?**
  For example, technical regulations, conformity assessment, rules of origin and inspections.

- **What procedural obstacles do exporters/importers encounter?**
  For example, delays and problems with recognizing certificates.

- **Where does the problem occur?**
  For example, at home or in the partner country, and the institutions or agencies involved.

The following chapters present the survey insights about trade obstacles among Arab States. Although these economies' exports are heavily oriented towards the EU, they account for a significant share – about one third – of intraregional exports, excluding minerals and arms (figure 2). The findings are therefore an important contribution to the ongoing discussion on greater integration among Arab States and the elimination of intraregional trade obstacles.

For the sake of simplicity, the analysis concentrates on exporters' perspectives. Occasionally, these are supplemented by insights and anecdotal evidence from interviews conducted with importers, but without resorting to comprehensive data analysis.[3] As for the research questions listed above, this publication focuses on the last four, excluding a detailed discussion of the sector, product or company differences affected by burdensome NTMs.[4]

---

3 Data on the importers' perspectives are available for Egypt, Morocco and Tunisia. In the State of Palestine, the survey focused exclusively on exporters.

4 More details are available on each economy in the respective NTM Survey reports. Three of these reports may be accessed from www.intracen.org/publications/ntm. The report for Egypt is forthcoming. NTM Survey results can also be consulted at www.ntmsurvey.org.

A SNAPSHOT OF NTM SURVEY FINDINGS

NTM Survey findings at a glance

- NTMs have a significant impact on exporters in Arab States.
- Regionally applied measures constitute a sizeable share of burdensome NTMs.
- Measures of conformity assessment and rules of origin stand out as particularly difficult to deal with.
- Problems with home-country export measures exacerbate existing trade obstacles.

- More problematic than NTMs themselves are related procedural obstacles, which increase the cost of compliance.
- 'Before-the-border problems with behind-the-border measures' – domestic impediments comprise a substantial share of reported obstacles.

NON-TARIFF MEASURES AFFECT EXPORTERS IN ARAB STATES

Around the globe, many companies are well prepared for dealing with non-tariff measures. Experience and company size play a role, as do the products exported and imported and the countries with which a company trades. Not all businesses find it difficult to comply with NTMs. The ITC NTM Survey methodology determines in the initial interview whether or not a company is affected by burdensome NTMs. These initial interviews, usually carried out by telephone, identify those companies that are affected and invite them to participate in face-to-face follow-up interviews to understand fully the nature of the problems they face.

In the four surveyed Arab States, 44% of all trading companies (comprising both exporters and importers) reported facing burdensome NTMs, including those applied within and outside the Arab region. This share is lower than in African countries, where 73% (West Africa[5]) and 64% (East Africa[6]) of companies reportedly faced NTM-related difficulties. However, caution needs to be exercised when comparing the share of 'affectedness' between countries and regions because of national differences in implementing the surveys. Cultural differences in survey responses are also important to consider, such as the willingness of companies to divulge business-related difficulties, particularly those involving local government agencies.

In addition, the share of 'affected' companies reveals little about the difficulty of intraregional trade, which may be much more cumbersome than the overall affectedness of 44% suggests.

MANY BURDENSOME NTMS AMONG REGIONAL TRADING PARTNERS

To shed further light on the difficulty of regional trade, figure 3 below summarizes the origin of 'challenging' NTMs reported by exporting companies in Arab States. For both the agricultural and manufacturing sectors, a significant share of challenging measures affecting exports – 24% and 21%, respectively – is applied by the home country. This is in line with the findings of NTM Surveys in other countries and regions, which show that many trade impediments originate at home.

Trade agreements on preferential market access hence do not insulate against NTM-related problems. Most burdensome NTMs in the four economies were reported to be applied by partner countries, in particular Arab States and EU member States, despite the existing free trade agreements.

In agriculture, more NTM cases concern the EU than Arab States (32% vs. 28%; figure 3, left). In manufacturing, the share of cases concerning Arab States is higher (37% vs. 15% for the EU; figure 3, right). For manufacturing, burdensome NTMs applied by partners outside the Arab world involve predominantly non-EU countries, such as Canada, Israel, Kenya, Switzerland and the United States.

These figures represent weighted averages, but differences between the four economies are pronounced. In line with its trade structure, Morocco reports far fewer cases related to Arab States than the average, and relatively more cases concerning the EU. The opposite holds true for Egypt. For the State of Palestine, an above-average number of cases concern NTMs applied by Israel (which is counted as part of the 'rest of the world'). This is a consequence of the

---

5   In West Africa, NTM Surveys were carried out in Burkina Faso, Côte d'Ivoire, Guinea and Senegal.
6   In East Africa, NTM Surveys were carried out in Kenya, Madagascar, Malawi, Mauritius, Rwanda and the United Republic of Tanzania.

Figure 3: Breakdown of burdensome NTM cases reported by exporters in Arab States

Agricultural   **Manufacturing**

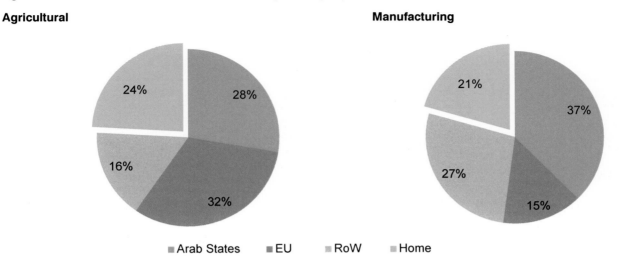

Source: ITC NTM Surveys in Egypt, Morocco, State of Palestine and Tunisia, 2010–2013.

The pie charts show that 28% of NTM cases reported by agricultural exporters concern measures applied by Arab States; 15% of burdensome NTMs on manufacturing exports are from EU countries.

sampling for the NTM Surveys, which is closely linked to the trade pattern of each country and therefore leads to a correlation between export shares and the number of NTM cases (for both sectors and partner countries).

In order to assess the perceived difficulty of different groups of trading partners, the reported NTM cases have therefore to be put into the trade context. Figure 4 plots the share of NTM cases against the share of exports by partner region. If the former exceeds the latter, a destination market can be said to be relatively difficult to access. The figure shows that relative to their importance as an export destination, Arab States are responsible for a disproportionate share

of reported cases of burdensome regulations. This is especially true of the manufacturing sector, for which only 16% of exports are destined to other Arab States but nearly half of the reported NTM cases concern measures applied by partner countries within the region. In contrast, other countries, particularly in the EU market, seem relatively accessible.

For agricultural exports, the share of NTM cases for RoW, which is lower than the share of exports, is driven by countries outside the EU. In fact, the European Union appears to be just as challenging a destination as Arab States for exporters of agricultural products. An outlier is Morocco, where no NTM

Figure 4: Burdensome NTM cases vs. export share

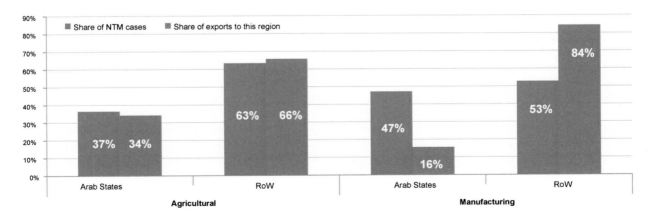

Source: ITC NTM Surveys on NTMs in Egypt, Morocco, State of Palestine and Tunisia, 2010–2013; and ITC staff calculations based on Trade Map data for 2013.

The figure shows that 37% of the burdensome NTMs reported by exporters of agricultural products in the surveyed Arab States are applied by regional trading partners, while only 34% of their exports go to the Arab region. For manufacturing, 47% of NTM cases concern Arab States' regulations, as compared with only 16% of exports.

Notes: Export shares are calculated excluding minerals and arms. Only burdensome NTMs reported by exporters are considered. Shares of NTM cases are weighted averages of the survey findings for Egypt, Morocco, State of Palestine and Tunisia.

Figure 5: Agricultural exports: burdensome NTMs applied by partner countries

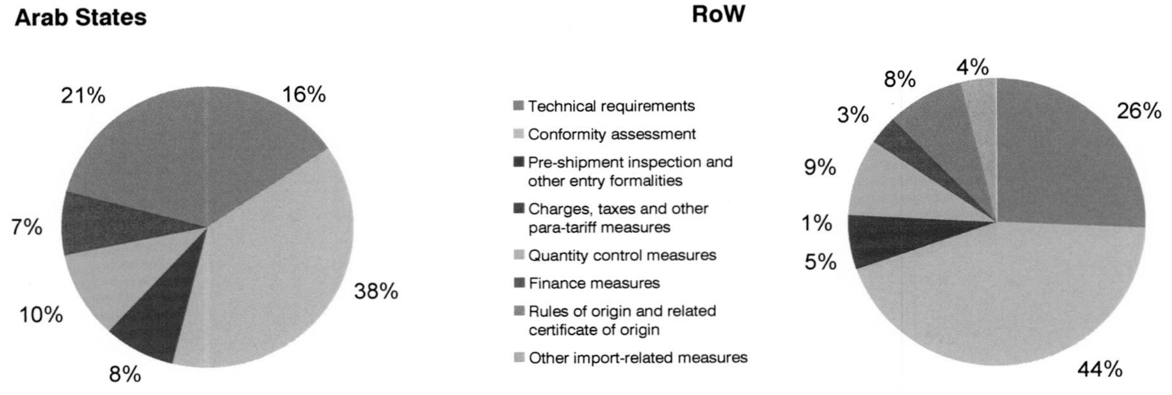

Arab States   **RoW**

Legend:
- Technical requirements
- Conformity assessment
- Pre-shipment inspection and other entry formalities
- Charges, taxes and other para-tariff measures
- Quantity control measures
- Finance measures
- Rules of origin and related certificate of origin
- Other import-related measures

Source: ITC NTM Surveys in Egypt, Morocco, State of Palestine and Tunisia, 2010–2013.

The pie charts indicate that 38% of the burdensome NTMs applied by Arab partner countries concern conformity assessment requirements.

case was reported by the very few companies that export agricultural products to other Arab States.

CHALLENGES: SPS, TBT, RULES OF ORIGIN

The types of burdensome NTMs experienced by companies when exporting agricultural products to other Arab States are summarized in figure 5 (left). Sanitary and phytosanitary (SPS) measures and technical barriers to trade (TBT) are perceived as the most challenging. More than half (54%) of the NTM cases fall into this category, which comprises:

- Technical regulations, i.e. product-specific requirements such as tolerance limits for residues, hygienic requirements or measures on labelling and packaging;
- Conformity assessment measures aimed at proving compliance with technical regulations, for example through testing and certification.

Companies have significantly more problems in complying with conformity assessment measures applied by regional partner countries than with technical regulations themselves. This holds true for all trading partners, whether they are within or outside the region (figure 5, right).

Rules of origin are another challenge for companies exporting agricultural products to other Arab countries. GAFTA and numerous bilateral agreements between Arab States have established tariff-free market access in principle. To benefit from tariff preferences, companies must prove their product origin. In this way, trade agreements replace the tariff with a non-tariff measure. This is not necessarily problematic. For example, for the EU, only 6% of reported NTM-related problems concern rules of origin, but these rules appear to be a major challenge when trading with other Arab States.

Other burdensome measures reported for Arab States include quantity control measures (licences, quotas etc.), charges and taxes, and finance measures (such as regulations on terms of payment for imports or on official foreign exchange allocation). Together, these measures represent 25% of challenging NTMs applied by Arab countries, in contrast to only 13% of such measures applied by countries outside the region.

Outside the League of Arab States (figure 5, right), quantity control measures for agricultural products are reported predominantly for the EU market. Problematic pre-shipment inspections (5%) primarily concern Israeli inspections of Palestinian exports.

NTMs reported by exporters in the manufacturing sector are displayed in figure 6. Compared with agricultural exporters, companies report fewer problems with SPS and TBT measures within the region. However, when compared with manufacturing exports to the rest of the world, particularly outside the EU, the incidence of SPS and TBT measures appears high.

Similarly, the challenges related to rules of origin are much more pronounced, when compared both with manufacturing exports outside the region (figure 6, right) and with agricultural exports (figure 5, right); 31% of NTM cases concern this type of measure. Finance measures and charges, together with taxes, are relatively more problematic for Arab trading partners than for partners in other regions.

Substantial differences exist among non-Arab export destinations. The EU accounts for most cases of burdensome technical requirements and, together with the United States, for most of the reported difficulties related to rules of origin. Burdensome pre-shipment inspections were reported mostly by Egyptian and Palestinian exporters in relation to Kenya (for Egypt) and Israel (for the State of Palestine).

Figure 6: Manufacturing exports: burdensome NTMs applied by partner countries

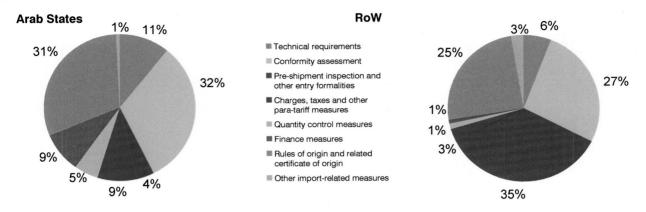

Arab States

1%
11%
31%
32%
9%
9%
5%
4%

RoW

3% 6%
25%
27%
1%
1%
3%
35%

- ■ Technical requirements
- ▨ Conformity assessment
- ■ Pre-shipment inspection and other entry formalities
- ■ Charges, taxes and other para-tariff measures
- ▨ Quantity control measures
- ■ Finance measures
- ▨ Rules of origin and related certificate of origin
- ▨ Other import-related measures

Source: ITC NTM Surveys in Egypt, Morocco, State of Palestine and Tunisia, 2010–2013.
The pie charts indicate that 31% of the burdensome NTMs applied by Arab export destinations concern rules of origin.

The NTM Survey findings from Egypt, Morocco, the State of Palestine and Tunisia suggest that intraregional trade in the Arab world, in particular for manufacturing products, is strongly affected by NTM-related trade obstacles. SPS and TBT measures as well as rules of origin are perceived as major challenges for exporting to other Arab countries. This is despite the fact that the GAFTA Agreement includes provisions for eliminating non-tariff barriers to trade.

MEASURES AT HOME CAN POSE CHALLENGES

As figure 3 indicates, partner-country regulations are not the only problems reported by exporters. A considerable number of burdensome NTMs concern export-related measures at home, notably export inspections, certification requirements, export taxes and charges, and licensing or registration requirements (figure 7). Other export-related measures include export quotas and export prohibitions.

PROCEDURAL OBSTACLES INCREASE COMPLIANCE COSTS

The NTM Surveys identify the root cause of NTM challenges for exporters. The surveys distinguish between measures considered 'too strict' (hard to comply with because of the measure itself); measures that are difficult to comply with due to procedural obstacles (such as administrative delays and inappropriate facilities); and measures that are both too strict and are associated with procedural obstacles. This distinction is vital for defining the appropriate response to the reported problems.

Figure 7: Burdensome NTMs applied at home

Agricultural

16%
20%
10%
7%
6%
10%
31%

Manufacturing

14%
4%
42%
21%
3%
7% 9%

- ■ Export inspection
- ▨ Certification required by the exporting country
- ▨ Other export technical measures
- ■ Export taxes and charges
- ▨ Licensing or permit to export
- ▨ Export registration
- ▨ Other export-related measures

Source: ITC NTM Surveys in Egypt, Morocco, State of Palestine and Tunisia, 2010–2013.
The figure shows that export inspections constitute 20% of burdensome NTMs applied at home on agricultural exports.

Figure 8: Why exporters find NTMs a burden

Agriculture

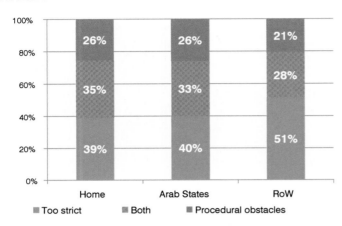

Manufacturing

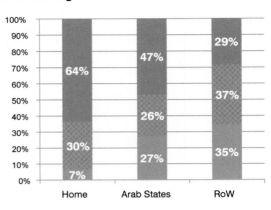

■ Too strict   ■ Both   ■ Procedural obstacles

Source: ITC NTM Surveys in Egypt, Morocco, State of Palestine and Tunisia, 2010–2013.

Procedural obstacles are a major concern. The charts show that 61% of NTMs applied at home on agriculture (left) and 94% of those applied on manufacturing products (right) are considered burdensome because of procedural obstacles.

In line with findings in other countries, the surveys suggest that most NTMs are not themselves problematic, especially for manufacturing products. Linked to the majority of non-tariff measures that are reported as challenging are procedural obstacles that render compliance with the underlying NTMs difficult, either as the only cause (shown by the grey sections of the bars in figure 8) or as contributing factors (shown by the dotted sections of the bars). For example, an exporter may be compliant with the required tolerance limit for pesticides, yet has difficulties in proving compliance because the accredited testing laboratory is too costly or far away.

Compared with the rest of the world, the incidence of procedural obstacles is higher for measures applied by Arab States and highest for measures applied at home.

For agricultural exports to Arab States, one fourth of the NTM cases would not have been reported if the procedural obstacles did not exist, and one third would be considered at least less onerous (figure 8, left). For manufacturing, the impact of procedural obstacles is even higher: Nearly one half of the problems related to NTMs were applied by regional trading partners, and nearly two thirds of those applied at home would be eliminated if the procedural obstacles were removed (figure 8, right).

This is a powerful message because it suggests that a considerable share of the obstacles to intraregional trade could be eliminated by tackling procedural obstacles – that is, by facilitating trade rather than changing the underlying trade rules.

Figure 9: Where exporters encounter procedural obstacles

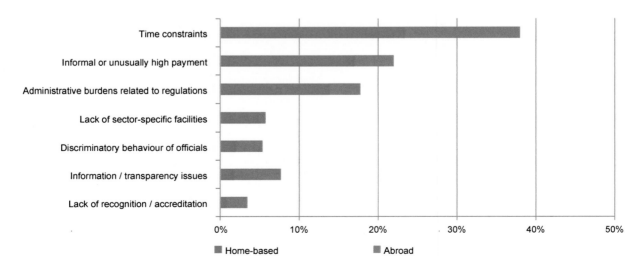

■ Home-based   ■ Abroad

Source: ITC NTM Surveys in Egypt, Morocco, State of Palestine and Tunisia, 2010–2013.

According to surveyed exporters, these procedural obstacles arise when trying to comply with measures applied by other Arab States (excluding home country measures). The figure shows that 38% of procedural obstacles concern time constraints (notably delays), with 23% at home and 15% in the partner country.

DOMESTIC IMPEDIMENTS – A LARGE SHARE OF REPORTED OBSTACLES

The procedural obstacles encountered by exporters in relation to NTMs applied by Arab States are summarized in figure 9. A significant share of partner-country measures is difficult to comply with because of home-based procedural obstacles (blue section of the bars, figure 9). These obstacles are primarily linked to bureaucracy (including delays associated with red tape), payments and lack of facilities (e.g. for testing). This is mirrored by the procedural obstacles reported in association with measures applied by the home country (not shown).

Procedural obstacles that frequently occur in partner countries include discriminatory behaviour of officials, problems arising from lack of information and transparency, and the lack of recognition of national certificates (figure 9).

The survey data also show where the home-based procedural obstacles arise (table 2). The customs authority is the agency most frequently mentioned for procedural obstacles. This is not surprising. All exporters must go through customs, whereas only some deal with the Ministry of Agriculture. The customs authority facilities are also where controls and inspections take place, even when carried out by other agencies. Exporters may perceive customs to be

Table 2: Procedural obstacles affecting exports in agencies at home and in Arab States, by type and institution

	Agency	Time constraints	Informal or unusually high payment	Administrative burdens related to regulations	Lack of sector-specific facilities	Information/ transparency issues	Discriminatory behaviour of officials	Lack of recognition / accreditation	Other procedural obstacles
At home	Customs authority or public institution in charge of export and import control								
	Laboratories for product testing and analysis								
	Ministry in charge of international trade								
	Chambers of commerce and trade support institutions/funds								
	Airport or port authority								
	Export and import inspecting company (private)								
	Ministry of Health								
	Ministry of Agriculture								
	Ministry of Finance								
	Other ministries								
	Other agencies								
	Other private companies/banks								
In the region	Customs authority or public institution in charge of export and import control								
	Laboratories for product testing and analysis								
	National authorities/embassy								
	Ministry of Health								
	Airport or port authority								
	Other agencies								
	Other private companies/banks								

Legend: The varying intensities of green–yellow and orange–red indicate the frequency with which procedural obstacles are mentioned for a given institution and type of procedural obstacle. Green is the lowest frequency and red is the highest. White indicates that no procedural obstacle is recorded.

Source: ITC NTM Surveys in Egypt, Morocco, State of Palestine and Tunisia, 2010–2013.

The table suggests that many obstacles involve the customs authority or any other public institution in charge of export/import control, and that chambers of commerce and other TISIs are often associated with administrative burdens.

the 'location' of a procedural obstacle, whether the authority acts merely as implementing agency or as the setting for other agencies' procedures.

In contrast to pre-shipment inspections carried out by public institutions – plagued predominantly by delays, lack of facilities (e.g. cooling or storage) and administrative burdens (such as a large number of documents) that affect the efficiency of customs clearance – those carried out by private companies are associated mainly with high cost.

Quality control and testing involving laboratories and standardization bodies are perceived as problematic due to the time and high cost of procedures, as well as the lack of testing facilities and accreditation of laboratories.

Ministries are mentioned mostly in association with delays and administrative burdens, notably linked to issuing licences and certificates, including certificates of origin. Similar procedural obstacles are reported for TISIs, funds and chambers of commerce, which are often involved in issuing certificates.

Table 2 focuses on the procedural obstacles reported by exporters. A similar picture emerges, however, when analysing the procedural obstacles reported by importers (not shown).

CHAPTER 3

PRODUCT QUALITY AND CONFORMITY

PRODUCT QUALITY AND CONFORMITY

In brief: product quality and conformity obstacles

- Insufficient private-sector capacity to comply with technical regulations;
- Difficult labelling requirements;
- Inefficient testing and certification procedures;
- High cost of certification;

- Lack of recognition of certificates and lack of harmonization;
- Lack of transparency of foreign standards and conformity assessment procedures;
- Lengthy product registration and import authorization procedures.

This chapter takes a closer look at the SPS and TBT measures that were highlighted previously as constituting a significant share of burdensome NTMs in intraregional trade in both the agriculture and the manufacturing sectors (figures 5 and 6).

When disaggregating the two broad categories of technical requirements and conformity assessment, three types of measures stand out as particularly problematic: product certification, testing, and labelling requirements (figure 10). The agencies associated with procedural obstacles involving technical NTMs are listed in table 3. Entities in charge of testing and certification are mentioned the most frequently.

The following sections discuss the problems related to companies' capacity to comply with technical regulations

(section 1); issues with product testing and certification (section 2); and company grievances about product registration and import authorization (section 3).

COMPLIANCE CHALLENGES WITH TECHNICAL REGULATIONS

Technical regulations comprise measures regulating product identity, quality and performance, labelling and other technical requirements (the first three categories in figure 10). Most of them are perceived as challenging because of their strictness. Only a few problems involve procedural obstacles, most of which concern the lack of

Figure 10: Burdensome technical NTMs applied by Arab States

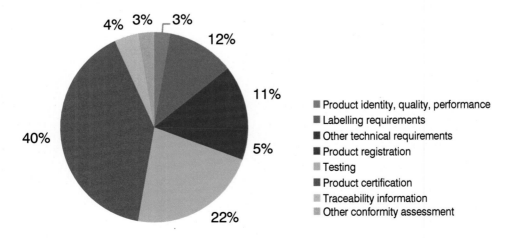

- Product identity, quality, performance
- Labelling requirements
- Other technical requirements
- Product registration
- Testing
- Product certification
- Traceability information
- Other conformity assessment

Source: ITC NTM Surveys in Egypt, Morocco, State of Palestine and Tunisia, 2010–2013.

The pie chart presents burdensome technical NTMs faced by companies in the surveyed economies when exporting to other Arab States. It represents a further breakdown of the first two categories of NTMs presented in figures 6 and 7 (technical requirements and conformity assessment) for all sectors. The pie chart shows that 22% of the burdensome technical NTMs applied by Arab export destinations concern testing requirements.

Table 3: Technical NTM-related procedural obstacles reported by exporters, by type and institution)

	Procedural obstacle → Agency	Time constraints	Informal or unusually high payment	Administrative burdens related to regulations	Lack of sector-specific facilities	Discriminatory behaviour of officials	Information/ transparency issues	Lack of recognition/ accreditation
At home	Testing/control/certification agencies							
	Ministry of Agriculture							
	Ministry of Health							
	Ministry in charge of international trade							
	TISIs and similar agencies							
	Private export and import inspecting company							
	Customs							
	Other agencies							
	Other private companies/banks							
In the region	Testing/control/certification agencies							
	Ministry of Health							
	Customs							

Legend: Green indicates the lowest frequency and red, the highest. White indicates that no procedural obstacle is recorded.

Source: ITC NTM Surveys in Egypt, Morocco, State of Palestine and Tunisia, 2010–2013.

The table shows that most obstacles involve testing and certification agencies at home, and that those obstacles concern mainly time constraints and high cost.

available information about foreign standards, frequently changing requirements and occasionally the high cost related to regulations (e.g. cost of fumigation).

Burdensome technical NTMs are generally reported more for countries outside the region than for other Arab States. Labelling requirements are a notable exception and will be discussed separately below.

TECHNICAL REQUIREMENTS (OTHER THAN LABELLING)

The reported cases cover the full spectrum of technical requirements, from fumigation, packaging and traceability to requirements for environmental protection, product safety and other technical specifications, as well as quality standards, including the requirement for some products to be halal.

Companies cite strict environmental standards for air conditioning, refrigerators and other electrical appliances; product safety measures 'that even clients don't ask for';· detailed traceability requirements, for example on an animal's health history; and details about the farm and the factory or the processing of raw materials, 'which is sometimes difficult to obtain with details'.

These comments point to serious deficiencies of the private sector in Arab States in understanding and complying with product quality requirements. While figure 10 suggests a relatively low incidence of such problems, it should be remembered that the NTM Surveys address active exporters – that is, those companies which have already succeeded in bringing products across the border. As a result, the numbers understate the dimension for the private sector as a whole, including non-exporting producers. Technical requirements such as those listed above may explain why many companies are unable to export in the first place.

The survey findings indicate a need to raise Arab companies' capacity to produce high-quality products and to improve the documentation of production processes and of ingredients' origin and composition (traceability). This would benefit trade in general, both within and beyond the region.

The findings also confirm that food exporters feel the consequences of (mostly temporary) import restrictions from Arab partner countries related to such diseases as avian flu, foot-and-mouth disease, swine flu and 'mad cow disease' (BSE).

LABELLING ISSUES STAND OUT

The relatively high frequency with which labelling is reported as problematic distinguishes the Arab NTM Survey findings from those of other countries. The problem is reported primarily for intraregional trade, compared with other technical regulations, more frequently mentioned for trade with countries outside the region.

Many companies struggle with strictly applied requirements due to the amount and level of detail on the label, as well as the way in which information should be presented. Another grievance is that labelling each item or small package complicates the production process. As with the issues involving other technical regulations, these problems are often rooted in companies' inexperience, their limited capacity to acquire information or their inability to adopt high-quality labelling.

'Labelling requirements are very strict.

'Once we had problems during customs clearance because the font on the label was one point smaller than the required size.'

Regional tomato exporter

Added to company-level problems are external factors that make labelling compliance a challenge. Companies complain about 'arbitrary' requirements, such as the obligation to indicate validity of only three months even if the actual product expiry date is several months later. Exporters also report that Arab countries, more than those in other regions, frequently change their labelling requirements, often with short notice or no notice at all.

Most important, from the regional integration perspective, are differing requirements between countries. Some countries require both the production date and the expiry date; others reject labels that indicate the production date. Some require detailed, specific information on applied standards. Some countries reject labels stating that a product is 'cholesterol-free', while others encourage them. Some require the name of the producing enterprise; others require the name of the client, in addition to or instead of the producing enterprise's name. Some accept stickers, while others request the labelling information to be irremovable, e.g. engraved in the packaging or on the product. Finally, differing language requirements pose problems.

To many companies, customizing labels to meet different and sometimes mutually exclusive requirements entails unnecessary incremental costs. At the same time, non-compliance with labelling requirements can turn out to be very costly in terms of fines – as much as $5,000 per shipment – or the rejection of a shipment at customs.

PRODUCT TESTING AND CERTIFICATION

Product testing and certification issues in the four NTM Surveys concern all types of conformity assessment procedures, including but not limited to residues testing, health certificates, veterinary certificates, and hazard analysis and critical control points (HACCP) certification.

Unlike technical requirements, product testing and certification procedures imposed by Arab partner countries are perceived as burdensome mainly because of procedural obstacles. Relatively few exporters complain about the strictness of the underlying regulations that require testing or certification. Reported problems concern 'double certification', i.e. requirements to obtain certificates from both the partner country and the home country, with the home country certificates required by the partner country as well. Other problems are the multitude of health or other quality certificates combined with what is perceived as excessive testing. These problems tend to arise with exports that compete with products in destination countries.

The majority of problems involve procedural obstacles and can be grouped into four categories: inefficient testing and certification procedures, high cost of certification, lack of recognition of certificates, and transparency issues.

INEFFICIENT TESTING AND CERTIFICATION PROCEDURES

Lengthy procedures

Testing and certification procedures are perceived as lengthy and complicated, which adds significantly to the time needed for exporting. Typically, the problems originate at home, where the certification required by partner countries is issued. Problems also occur at the border,

'Sometimes the importing country or the customers require a certificate based on a specific test that can be performed only by our national organization for standardization and quality.

'The testing process starts after the production of the whole shipment is completed. It takes from 30 to 60 days, but the validity of the product is just a year.

'Testing is very expensive, which discourages us from exporting because we want to avoid losses.'

Regional processed-food exporter

where products are sometimes retested upon entry into the partner country, which then delays customs clearance (see Chapter 4 on customs). In a few instances, among others reported for Saudi Arabia, the samples need to be sent directly to the partner country.

The delay depends on the country, the product, the institution involved and the type of test or certificate required. It is difficult to generalize, but the survey findings provide anecdotal evidence. Exporters sometimes wait several weeks for certificates to be issued and face from four to 10 additional days for customs clearance due to unforeseen additional testing.

The unpredictability of the delay is a bigger problem for exporters than the length of the delay because it impedes effective business planning and causes difficulties, especially with less established customers.

Frequent renewal of certification

Frequent renewal of test results and certification poses problems. This is especially burdensome when import authorization and product registration requirements are very thorough and take several months to complete. For example, the requirement to renew product quality certification annually is perceived as overly burdensome.

Excessive paperwork, numerous administrative windows

Excessive paperwork adds to the lengthiness of testing and certification procedures. Often a number of different entities, including laboratories and ministries, are involved in providing test results and issuing certification. In some instances, exporters must obtain certificates from both the Ministry of Agriculture and the Ministry of Health in order to satisfy Arab partner-country requirements. These certificates must then be legalized by the Ministry of Foreign Affairs before they can be presented to the relevant authorities of the partner country for import authorization, product registration or customs clearance. Exporters in the surveyed economies find the often-missing coordination between the different entities deplorable. This lack of coordination produces delays and a heavy administrative burden, including duplication of paperwork, which is difficult to shoulder – especially for smaller companies.

'The problem? It's the quantity of papers to submit.

'There are too many documents needed to prepare the dossier. More than 20 different documents are required for the conformity assessment process.'

Regional exporter of gas water heaters

Insufficient, inaccessible or absent infrastructure

Where adequate electronic systems and procedures are lacking, producers are often required to go in person to the capital to obtain certain types of certifications. This particularly affects exporters who are based far from the capital. Problems also arise where the capacity of the accredited laboratory or laboratories is limited, which leads to processing delays.

Access to existing national infrastructure may be challenging, but a complete lack of infrastructure is a monumental trade obstacle. In all four surveyed economies, numerous exporters report problems arising from a lack of expertise in the country, lack of appropriate laboratory facilities or equipment, lack of accreditation of existing laboratories or lack of recognition of issued certificates (see below for more information about certificates).

The severity of these infrastructure issues differs among the economies, with the State of Palestine being particularly affected. It also depends on the products and the export destination. The problems increase with the complexity or specificity of the testing required. Missing infrastructure is not a problem specific to intraregional trade. Currently, it has a greater impact on trade with partners outside the region, and particularly with members of the Organisation for Economic Co-operation and Development (OECD), which tend to have stricter and more complex quality requirements. However, as the Arab world seeks to enhance product quality standards for the benefit of consumers, the importance of these infrastructure-related problems in intraregional trade will undoubtedly persist and multiply.

HIGH CERTIFICATION COSTS

For many exporters, certification and testing costs are serious obstacles. Reported fees and costs vary widely. The smaller the company, and the smaller the size and value of shipments, the more increases in fees and costs (however slight) are perceived as problematic.

For example, a 'weed-free product certificate' for beans is reported to cost US$ 140 per shipment; US$ 267 per shipment is the cost of conformity certification of plastic tubes, which according to one exporter is 'a certification that is granted without prior inspections'.

Fees for radioactivity and bacteria tests imposed by one Arab State on food imports, with the test to be undertaken in the destination country, amount to US$ 800 per shipment. For exports to another country, which accepts locally issued certificates, the cost of similar certification is US$ 100. The cost of certifying a product against EN 817, a standard for sanitary tap ware, can reportedly exceed US$ 4,000 per shipment.

'The partner country requires that products should be free of genetically modified organisms and dioxin. Our Ministry of Health is unable to test the products and issue the relevant certificate because of the lack of appropriate facilities or equipped labs.

'We overcome this problem by testing the products internally and authenticating the results with the chamber of commerce. This is accepted because our company is ISO 22000 certified.'

Regional processed-food exporter

Costs further increase when insufficient public infrastructure forces companies to turn to private service providers such as SGS, or testing facilities abroad, for example in Israel (notably in the case of the State of Palestine) or Europe. A fee of US\$ 570 for testing organic soap can be a major setback to a Palestinian exporter's competitiveness. In one case, an exporter of basic manufacturing reported incurring US\$ 30,000 in costs and fees for testing products in the Netherlands.

LACK OF RECOGNITION OF CERTIFICATES AND HARMONIZATION

Conformity assessments, such as the exporters' ISO 22000 certification above, will not help if they are not recognized by the partner country. Incidences of non-recognition have been reported for ISO 22000 and a variety of other certificates. This occurs despite the existence of GAFTA and, at times, explicit mutual recognition agreements between two Arab States, for example, the State of Palestine and Jordan.

The great variety of quality standards applied across the Arab world, and differences in the types and number of certificates needed for a particular product and partner country, make exporting to more than one destination onerous in terms of:

- Carrying out the tests – either different tests or the same tests by different entities, depending on what is recognized;

'The destination country's customs authority requires a conformity certificate from its national standards body. Any equivalent or accredited certification from our national laboratory is never recognized or accepted.

'The certification process is usually delayed for three to four days, which could damage sensitive products that need refrigeration.'

Regional cheese exporter

- Providing the related certificates – excessive paperwork;
- Satisfying differing product quality requirements for different destinations.

LACK OF TRANSPARENCY OF FOREIGN STANDARDS AND CONFORMITY ASSESSMENT PROCEDURES

Access to information is a theme cutting across all types of non-tariff measures. Inadequately published or frequently changing standards and certification requirements, often without due notice of changes, means that exporters may not become aware of certain requirements until they actually reach the border. This is inefficient from all perspectives. Exporters incur high costs when shipments are delayed or denied entry altogether. Customs authorities face bottlenecks in clearance due to 'unprepared' exporters and possibly limited storage facilities. Organizations in charge of testing are under pressure to provide results quickly to unblock shipments. Customers face unpredictable delays in receiving the goods, assuming they wait at all.

Inadequate dissemination of requirements can lead to confusion, or to exporters being unable to verify or contest ambiguous regulations, as in the case of a processed-food exporter who was required to have certificates that typically apply only to manufactured products.

There is also a lack of information about the certification entities and procedures in the home country. Companies

'The partner country's authorities require that the company should hold ISO 14001 certification [on environmental management], which is difficult to obtain.

'Information on this requirement was not well publicized. We therefore missed the opportunity to export to this country.'

Regional furniture exporter

complain they do not know which designated authority provides recognized certification and do not know the procedure to obtain internationally recognized certification. They also object to the high costs involved.

PRODUCT REGISTRATION AND IMPORT AUTHORIZATION

Burdensome product registration and import authorization requirements applied by Arab States are reported primarily for pharmaceuticals and other chemicals, electrical appliances and agricultural products. In some countries, particularly in the Gulf region, procedures are perceived to be very strict and are prohibitive for some exporters.

'Product registration is very difficult and must be renewed every two years. The registration process itself is usually delayed for almost one year and is relatively expensive – US$ 2,850 – per product.'

Regional electrical appliances exporter

Like product certification and testing, these procedures suffer from lack of transparency, high costs and significant delays –frequently reported to exceed one year. The need to re-register annually or biennially adds to the complexity and time constraints.

Many companies, particularly smaller firms and occasional exporters, are overwhelmed by the amount of product details, including on packaging and labelling, and of papers that must be submitted to register or obtain import authorization. In one case, an exporter claimed procedures were 'biased and difficult because the guidelines are tailored and customized to fit a European competitor'.

'After complying with the strict technical specifications, we should have received an import authorization, but it has been delayed for more than five months already.'

Regional television exporter

Even when registration is complete and authorization obtained, products are reportedly held up often at the border for lengthy periods of time to 'verify' registration and authorization status.

CHAPTER 4

RULES OF ORIGIN AND OTHER TRADE-RELATED MEASURES

RULES OF ORIGIN AND OTHER TRADE-RELATED MEASURES

In brief: Obstacles involving rules of origin and other trade-related measures

- Rules of origin:
    - De jure vs. de facto preferential treatment;
    - Language issues;
    - Inefficiency in issuing the certificates of origin;
    - GAFTA, Israel and (other) problems related to 'made in Palestine';
- Terms of payment and other finance measures;

- Consular invoice fees, taxes and other charges levied on imports;
- Quantity control measures and protectionism in disguise;
- 'Home-made' problems: export taxes, registration, licensing and unintended adverse effects of export support mechanisms.

This chapter examines non-technical measures that hamper intra-Arab trade, as reported by surveyed exporters. Figure 11 provides details for NTM categories 3–8 (from pre-shipment inspection to rules of origin), which are presented in figures 5 and 6 for both the manufacturing and agricultural sectors combined.

The institutions that exporters associate with procedural obstacles involving non-technical NTMs are listed in table 4. The ministry in charge of international trade tends to be mentioned most frequently in connection with these issues, while customs authorities of partner countries are most frequently referred to when it comes to customs clearance and border controls.

RULES OF ORIGIN

Rules of origin pose a major problem for intraregional trade. They are mentioned more frequently in relation to trade with other Arab States than with OECD countries, particularly EU member States. The surveyed Arab States enjoy preferential treatment granted by EU member States, provided the exporter can deliver evidence of product origin. The following types of problems recur: failure to grant preferential treatment, language issues, inefficiency in issuing the certificates of origin, and specific problems related to 'made in Palestine'.

Figure 11: Burdensome non-technical NTMs applied in the region

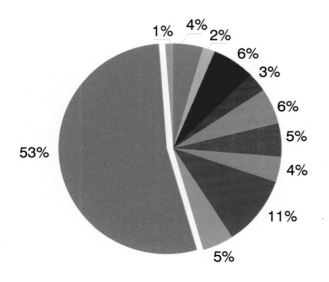

■	Pre-shipment inspection
■	Other entry formalities
■	Consular invoice fee
■	Internal taxes and charges levied on imports
■	Other taxes
■	Seasonal quotas
■	Other quantity measures
■	Regulations concerning terms of payment for imports
■	Other finance measures
■	Rules of origin and related certificate of origin
■	Other import-related measures

Source: ITC NTM Surveys in Egypt, Morocco, State of Palestine and Tunisia, 2010–2013.
The pie chart shows that 11% of the burdensome non-technical NTMs applied by Arab export destinations concern regulations on terms of payment.

Table 4: Incidence of procedural obstacles related to non-technical NTMs reported by exporters, by type and institution

	Agency / Type of procedural obstacle	Time constraints	Informal or unusually high payment	Administrative burdens related to regulations	Lack of sector-specific facilities	Discriminatory behaviour of officials	Information/ transparency issues	Lack of recognition/ accreditation	Other procedural obstacles
At home	Testing/control/certification agencies	▨	▨	▨	▨				
	Ministry of Agriculture								
	Ministry of Health								
	Ministry in charge of international trade	▨	▨						
	TISIs and similar agencies	▨	▨	▨			▨	▨	
	Export and import inspecting company	▨	▨					▨	
	Customs	▨							
	Other agencies	▨	▨						
	Other ministries	▨							
	Airport/port authority		▨						
	Other private companies/banks								
In the region	Customs	▨	▨	▨	▨	▨	▨	▨	▨
	Airport/port authority	▨			▨				

Legend: The varying intensities of green–yellow and orange–red indicate the frequency of procedural obstacles reported for a given institution and type of procedural obstacle, with green being the lowest and red the highest frequency. White indicates that no procedural obstacle is recorded for the given pair of procedural obstacle and agency.

Source: ITC NTM Surveys in Egypt, Morocco, State of Palestine and Tunisia, 2010–2013.

The table presents the procedural obstacles related to the non-technical NTMs applied by Arab States to exports from the surveyed economies according to the location – at home or in the partner country – and type of obstacle. It shows that most obstacles occur in or involve the customs authority of the partner country, and that these obstacles mainly concern time constraints.

DE JURE VS. DE FACTO PREFERENTIAL TREATMENT

Numerous exporters observe that despite compliance with rules of origin under any or all of the agreements governing trade between two respective Arab States – typically GAFTA, the Agadir Agreement or the Common Market for Eastern and Southern Africa (COMESA) – companies are not granted preferential treatment and are obliged to pay tariffs.

Companies cite arbitrary decisions taken by officials at the point of entry into the partner country. According to exporters, such decisions are often the result of customs officials' lack of knowledge about the different origin requirements, especially when more than one agreement is in force. For example, officials may be uncertain whether a product complies with the rules stipulated in the Pan-Euro-Med origin protocol, which is in force between a number

'Although the products comply with GAFTA rules of origin, we always pay tariffs when exporting to specific Arab markets and are not granted the promised preferential treatment.'

'The partner country doesn't apply both existing agreements although the product satisfies the rules of origin. The situation forces us to pay tariffs. This inflates the prices charged to the consumer, and for some products it becomes unprofitable to export. This limited our opportunity in this market.'

Regional sugar confectionary and electrical appliance exporters of Arab States. As a result, they may refuse products containing inputs from China or any other country outside the Euro-Med zone, despite sufficient value addition for the product to be considered as originating in the exporting country. Even when the legal status is clear, if the customs official is uncertain, the preference is often not granted.

The situation is further complicated by incompatible or unclear requirements under the different agreements that are in force concurrently. Exporters cite problems with the Pan-Euro-Med origin certificate being refused on the basis of the Agadir Agreement, although in theory the same certificate should work under both agreements. They note that certain certificates are accepted only if accompanied by additional text. However, adding such text leads to refusals by other countries. Differing rules of origin thus cause confusion as to which agreement is actually binding.

For example, the origin requirements for Egyptian products are stricter under COMESA than under GAFTA. It is often unclear both to exporters and to customs officials how to deal with products that comply with GAFTA but not COMESA. Discussions with customs officials in one surveyed economy suggest that more recent agreements take precedence over older ones, with the date of the agreement's entry into force being the defining factor. This would mean that the provisions agreed under GAFTA can in theory be undermined if two countries agree bilaterally on stricter rules of origin at a later date, regardless of whether this is in keeping with the desire for greater regional integration. The predominant grievance remains the apparent lack of knowledge – both among companies and among customs officials – about which rule is in force and which certificate is to be presented or accepted.

Similarly, existing negative lists of products that do not qualify limit the de facto application of preferential treatment, either because some products are excluded from preferential trade or, as explained above, because they are considered differently under each agreement. Companies are not always sure whether exclusions pertain to official requirements or whether these are random negative lists. Anecdotal evidence suggests that some products may be excluded from preferential trade because the rules of origin are unclear.

> 'For GAFTA, the zero tariff rate has been applied for the past few years, but only for goods whose rules of origin are agreed upon.'
>
> Customs official commenting during ITC's tariff data collection

Unclear regulations pose difficulties as they create a margin of interpretation for customs officials, which means that companies confront different decisions depending on who they are dealing with. Vague guidelines in some countries on how exactly the origin is to be indicated on each product are one such example. In some instances, disputes arise between exporters and customs officials over the definition

and calculation of 'value addition', which is particularly important in determining manufacturing products' origins.

Preferential treatment is often not granted because of mistakes on the certificate or in the evidence to be provided as annexes. Many companies complain about the strictness with which the forms are scrutinized. Forms are sometimes rejected because of 'minor mistakes' such as typos. Lack of information on how to fill out the forms correctly is often cited as well.

Finally, the rules themselves are difficult to comply with for some exporters, in particular requirements on minimum value addition in manufactured products, which some consider overly restrictive. According to some of the interviews, this leads exporters unnecessarily to increase the product's end price – either because of an artificially inflated sales price to keep the percentage of the value of non-originating inputs in the final product below the required threshold, or because of the tariff that will have to be paid if the origin requirement is not met.

LANGUAGE ISSUES

Language requirements for the certificate of origin are an unexpected recurrent problem. This issue is unique to intraregional trade and is seldom reported for other destination countries, such as EU trading partners.

A number of countries require the GAFTA certificate of origin, and sometimes all enclosed bills and other evidence, to be '100% in Arabic'; otherwise the certificate is refused. Exporters, notably those of manufacturing products, claim that many technical specifications, letters or numbers cannot be translated or can be translated only imperfectly, which often results in significant expenditures in terms of time and cost. For example, a Tunisian exporter reported a cost of about US$ 38 per document, while others cited a cost of nearly US$ 100.

> 'When exporting to any Arab country and issuing a GAFTA certificate of origin, the certificate must be 100% in Arabic. There are some technical wordings, letters and numbers that cannot be translated. Customs officials do not understand this point and usually reject the certificate.'
>
> Regional compressors exporter

INEFFICIENCY IN ISSUING CERTIFICATES OF ORIGIN

Administrative inefficiencies are another reason why compliance with rules of origin is reported as burdensome. In all the surveyed economies, exporters deplore time-consuming procedures and lack of information about which agency to contact and what type of documentation to provide. This is especially hard for first-time exporters.

'At least two days…'

'Two weeks to prepare the documents to be submitted; five days to receive the certificate.'

'Between one week and 10 days only for issuance.'

'Three–four additional days because I have to go to the capital.'

'Around 13 days…

'Twenty days.'

'Two–three months to prepare the dossier. It's a waste of time and it's repetitive.'

Arab exporters commenting on
how long it takes to obtain the certificate of origin

Unpredictability of delays is a challenge, too. Because certificates are issued much later than expected or promised, products may be held up at the production site, the home border or the port of destination, resulting in delays in shipment and demurrage fees.

Delays in obtaining certificates of origin are aggravated by the paperwork that accompanies certification requests, with many exporters citing unnecessary duplication and at times differing demands depending on the day or the official in charge. Delays are often reported when more than one institution is involved in the process due to limited coordination among them.

Companies also struggle with the limited validity of certificates in terms of time or number of shipments, which obliges them to reapply frequently for certification – usually by resubmitting the same documents. The main problem with reapplication lies in the cost, which often includes fees for obtaining original documents or providing notarized copies.

In addition, the cost of the certificate itself is often reported as too high, especially for smaller exporters.

'Five–six documents.'

'At least 10 documents.'

'Ten different documents, every time.'

'Fifteen different documents.'

Arab exporters commenting on how many documents they
must provide for certificates of origin

ISSUES RELATED TO 'MADE IN PALESTINE'

The GAFTA Agreement stipulates that in order to benefit from preferential treatment, products should not have any component of Israeli origin. Some countries request a certificate from the shipping company to prove that the vessel did not pass through an Israeli port. These requirements may have been put in place to achieve common political objectives in the region, and possibly to support the 'Palestinian cause'. However, they are likely to have unintended and unexpected adverse effects on regional trade integration in general, and on the possibility for the State of Palestine to export to the Arab world in particular.

The requirement itself can be difficult to comply with. This is of particular concern to companies in the State of Palestine, where the vast majority of imports are sourced from Israel. This impediment will only increase as the State of Palestine attempts to diversify its exports away from products with no or low value addition – for example, from raw agricultural products towards more sophisticated manufacturing products, which require raw materials that are locally unavailable. In many cases, inputs originating in Israel cannot be sourced with similar ease and cost from elsewhere. As a result, exporting to other Arab States will become increasingly difficult for the State of Palestine because of (rather than 'despite') the GAFTA Agreement.

'According to GAFTA, originating products shouldn't have any Israeli components. The customs authorities in some importing countries require the presentation of many documents and declarations to prove that this requirement is fulfilled.

'A certificate from the shipping line is required, stating that the ship didn't pass through any Israeli port, which is really unnecessary. The other documents are difficult to obtain.'

Regional electronic components exporter

A vicious circle develops when companies exporting to the State of Palestine have their products treated as if they were being exported to Israel rather than the State of Palestine, for example when complying with the requirement to pass through specific ports, such as Ashdod. The exporters' concern is that as a result, preferential treatment is not granted because Israel is not a party to the GAFTA Agreement. The problem for the Palestinian importer may be that the product serves as an input to the production of a good destined for export, and it may be challenging to prove the actual origin of the input if it is considered a 're-export' from Israel.

Even when Israeli inputs are not used in the product being exported, they are suspected. Surveyed Palestinian exporters lament the explicit lack of trust of other Arab States in Palestinian product origin. Even when products are 100% 'made in Palestine' and accompanied by the appropriate certificate of origin, many Arab countries suspect Israeli inputs and refuse to grant preferential treatment. This is aggravated by suspicions that products which originate entirely in Israel or in the Israeli settlements in Palestinian territories may be falsely labelled as 'made in Palestine' so as to circumvent import restrictions.

In this instance, the product traceability requirements mentioned in the previous chapter become vital and immensely cumbersome for Palestinian exporters – not for reasons of quality, but due to difficulty in documenting the product origin.

Finally, for some Arab countries, the GAFTA rules of origin directly contradict provisions under other trade agreements with countries outside the region that require a specified minimum of inputs of Israeli origin to be granted preferential treatment. This is, for example, the case of some bilateral agreements with the United States. Contradictory provisions like these force exporters to choose between focusing on either intraregional or extraregional trade.

OTHER TRADE-RELATED MEASURES

Other NTMs reported as burdensome by exporters in the surveyed Arab States include partner-country measures on finance, especially terms of payment (constituting 16% of

> 'If we write on a product 'made in Palestine', we can't send it [due to problems with inspections].
>
> 'If we write on it (or our customers believe it to be) 'made in Israel', they don't buy it.'
>
> Regional exporter from State of Palestine

reported cases of non-technical NTMs), taxes and charges (15%) and quantity control measures (9%, figure 11), as well as a number of measures imposed by the home country on exports, such as export taxes or registration and licensing requirements (figure 7).

TERMS OF PAYMENT AND OTHER FINANCE MEASURES

Finance measures regulating terms of payment are perceived as a major obstacle when exporting to selected Arab countries, including Algeria, Libya, Sudan and the Syrian Arab Republic.

The surveyed exporters report that one country allows payment only through a letter of credit, supposedly to 'monitor and be in control of all trade transactions'. This increases the cost of the transaction due to administrative burdens and significant delays. Banks reportedly delay transfers intentionally, even when provided with a complete set of documents. Delays ranging from several months to two years are reported. Some exporters say they receive the letter of credit only when the shipment of the goods is confirmed to be under way.

In other countries, the fact that letters of credit are not accepted poses a problem. At the same time, restrictions on foreign exchange transactions can delay payments or prevent exports altogether.

Direct bank transfers between Arab States can be difficult or impossible, forcing buyers to pay in advance or to route the money through third countries. Some companies report delays in transfers of up to 45 days. In some instances, importers have to travel to the border or to the exporting country to pay in cash.

> 'Opening letters of credit through correspondent banks is very difficult and is usually delayed for almost two months. But it is the most secure way to trade with the partner country.'
>
> Regional manufacturing products exporter

CONSULAR FEES, TAXES AND OTHER CHARGES FOR IMPORTS

Another recurrent intraregional trade concern is the need to legalize all types of documentation, such as invoices, certificates of origin or sanitary certificates, at the destination country's local embassy or consulate. This is a time-consuming undertaking (up to 10 days). In addition, fees are charged for this legalization procedure (e.g. US$ 35 per document), which exporters perceive as unnecessary, particularly in light of the GAFTA Agreement.

Other fee-related impediments are para-tariff measures, such as high 'sales' or 'profit' taxes being imposed only on imported goods, while domestic producers pay lower rates or nothing.

Exporters also point to 'arbitrary additional taxes and charges', sometimes amounting to US$ 3,000 per shipment. These taxes and charges are levied without prior notice and with insufficient breakdown, and the amounts often differ from the information disseminated through websites or other official sources.

Reference pricing and other issues related to customs valuation and reclassification of products under different codes of the Harmonized Commodity Description and Coding System (the internationally standardized system

'To our knowledge, according to GAFTA, export documents do not need to be legalized.

'But the destination countries' customs authorities require that the invoice and other export documents be legalized through the payment of fees to embassies.'

Regional processed-food exporter

of names and numbers to classify traded products) can magnify the impact of ad valorem fees and taxation. Exporters claim that products are reclassified solely for the purpose of collecting more tariff revenues. At times, these para-tariff measures outweigh the advantages gained from a preferential tariff rate, if one is even obtained.

QUANTITY CONTROL AND PROTECTIONISM IN DISGUISE

Burdensome quantity control measures are responsible for about 9% of reported cases of regionally applied non-technical NTMs. They tend to concern agricultural rather than manufacturing products, and nearly all are considered too strict. Unlike other measures, such as the charges and taxes discussed above or rules of origin and related certification procedures that suffer from opaqueness, these measures seem to be fairly well publicized and known to exporters.

Reported measures include seasonal quotas, import licensing and outright import bans. From the exporters' perspective, most if not all of them serve to protect domestic production from foreign competition. Exporters suspect that regional partner countries intentionally complicate and delay import procedures for the same reason.

Regional trade is also affected by requirements to use national providers for shipping or other types of services. Protection of intellectual property rights is cited as yet another challenge to regional trade.

'HOME-MADE' PROBLEMS

The discussion of trade-related measures would not be complete without considering the national business environment, especially those requirements which countries impose on their own exporters. As figure 3 shows, concerns about these measures account for a sizeable share of reported problems that make it difficult to reach the home border. Import-related measures affect the ease of crossing the border to enter the partner country.

These challenges highlight the fact that market access begins at home. Trade facilitation can, and to a large extent should, also happen at home, independent from partner-country commitments at the bilateral, regional or international

'A domestic producer in a destination country copied our design and used a similar name, which he then registered under his own name.

'Now our products are perceived as violating intellectual property rights and are banned from entering the country. This is unfair.

'We had a well-established market share for this product for more than seven years. This measure is imposed to protect the national industry.'

Regional plastic products exporter

level. They also underscore the role of transparency and access to trade-related information.

Home-based measures cited in the surveys include export permits, registration or licensing requirements, and export taxes. They are typically considered burdensome because of procedural obstacles, such as:

- Complicated administrative procedures;
- The time involved in obtaining all permits and licences, with typical waiting times of several weeks or months;
- The requirement to renew permits or registration frequently, which means that companies cannot export during the renewal process;
- Arbitrary calculation of taxes, which differ from what is published in official sources.

Many exporters, especially inexperienced ones, are confused as to where to start – for example, which certificate or licence to apply for first, and where to apply. The combination of home-based and foreign requirements makes the export process a real challenge. Information about the types and number of documents required is inadequately disseminated. Evolving responsibilities of ministries and different departments within

'A valid industrial registration is required to export, and must be renewed annually.

'Renewal is only possible after expiry and is usually delayed for at least a month.'

Regional manufacturing products exporter

ministries cause further complications. As a result, customs officials are often confronted with exporters who 'start at the wrong end' of the process by coming to the border with incomplete or inadequate documentation.

The NTM Survey findings also underscore the importance of the national business environment as a factor that can either enable or disable trade. Reported issues include:

- The lack of security in ports, where the goods may be exposed to robbery and theft;
- Poor transport infrastructure within countries and the lack of direct transport routes between countries;
- Insufficient space on air carriers for merchandise transport, which encourages them to serve only a few large companies, request smaller shipments or pay bribes;
- Lack of computerized processes;
- Insufficient support to exporting companies in terms of access to finance, information and counselling.

Export support programmes exist, including drawback schemes, temporary exemption systems, training activities and support funds. However, such programmes are occasionally undermined by administrative inefficiencies to such an extent that the intended support becomes a burden.

Egypt's export development fund is one example. Exporters cite the large number of required documents, which are neither adequately publicized nor adequately disseminated; procedures that change frequently, and without prior notice; difficulties in obtaining the required documents; and excruciatingly slow administration. As a result, companies receive support only after a considerable investment of time and effort, usually involving delays ranging from six months to one or two years, and sometimes they receive no support at all.

'For our company to export directly under our name, we must undertake a type of "export registration". To issue or renew this licence, we must send an employee to a training programme.

'This does not result in better skills. It appears to be a measure intended just to collect money. We have stopped participating in the training and will be unable to export directly in future.'

Regional wood products exporter

CHAPTER 5

CUSTOMS CLEARANCE AND BORDER CONTROLS

CUSTOMS CLEARANCE AND BORDER CONTROLS

In brief: Obstacles in customs clearance and with border controls

- Inappropriate infrastructure and lack of high-performing facilities;
- Issues with the availability and training of officials;
- Frequently changing procedures and inadequate dissemination of information about customs clearance and related documents;

- Insufficient coordination between agencies within a country and between countries;
- The result: lengthy, bureaucratic and costly customs clearance.

Customs authorities or other border control agencies are mandated to collect revenue (tariffs and taxes) and to ensure that the safety and quality of imported goods conform to national standards. As such, customs clearance and border control procedures involve all types of non-tariff measures beyond those explicitly labelled 'pre-shipment inspections' (the first two categories in figure 12) or 'export inspections' (figure 7), including also the NTMs discussed in the previous two chapters (figures 10 and 11).

This makes customs authorities probably the most important agency in trade facilitation. Their basic challenge is to fulfil the mandate of revenue collection and product quality and safety control, while also ensuring a smooth import and export process. Private-sector demands for efficient and quick procedures thus need to be carefully weighed against the need to ensure that only those products which are in conformity with national legislation actually enter a country.

Figure 12: Burdensome inspection requirements applied by Arab States to exports from the surveyed economies as a share of all reported non-technical NTMs

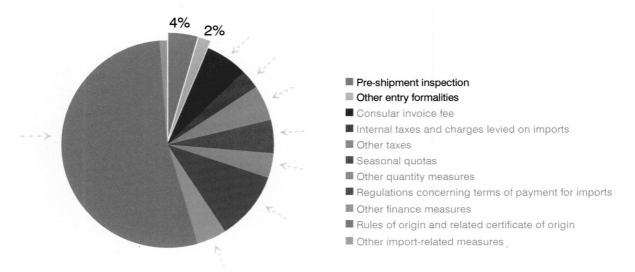

Source: ITC NTM Surveys in Egypt, Morocco, the State of Palestine and Tunisia, 2010–2013.

The pie chart presents burdensome non-technical NTMs faced by companies in the surveyed economies when exporting to other Arab States. It covers both agricultural and manufacturing sectors. It shows that 6% of the burdensome non-technical NTMs applied by Arab export destinations concern such measures. However, customs clearance and border control procedures affect all types of NTMs, both non-technical and technical (figure 10).

The NTM Survey findings generally suggest a number of opportunities in this regard, as most of the concerns reported about customs clearance are procedural obstacles that can be eliminated without compromising the primary objectives of customs authorities. In many ways, these issues mirror the problems highlighted in the last section of the previous chapter. One of the very few instances where companies question the inspection rule itself involves the lack of risk management systems and the resulting requirement for '100% inspections', which is the obligation to check each shipment thoroughly, without taking into consideration the number of exporters' or importers' transactions and their track record of 'reliability'.

INFRASTRUCTURE

Inappropriate infrastructure is a significant challenge for exporters and importers with respect to customs clearance. Companies are faced with outdated scanners and scanners of limited size and capacity, which substantially delay inspections as they limit the amount of exports that can be handled in a day. As a result, border stations sometimes explicitly limit the size of shipments allowed, which exporters and their customers find irritating if they wish to ship or purchase greater quantities.

> *'Products exported by air require an X-ray inspection to protect against explosives and smuggled goods. The X-ray devices are very limited and outdated, which usually delays the export clearance procedure and makes for a very expensive inspection.'*
>
> Regional oranges exporter

Storage facilities needed by companies awaiting customs clearance appear to be missing, ill-equipped (for example, for products that require cooling) or too expensive. Some companies say they resort to bribes in order to speed up inspections and avoid storage complications.

Finally, exporters and importers complain that in many countries electronic submission of documents is either impossible or slow, that the process lacks user-friendliness and that the system is subject to frequent breakdowns.

AVAILABILITY AND TRAINING OF OFFICIALS

The 'hardware' problems described above are compounded by difficulties with personnel. Companies report limited service hours and shortages in the number of staff available to carry out the different tasks involved in inspections and

> *'The customs official who comes to seal the shipments is often not available due to absence or vacations. We then have to wait for a replacement to arrive, which takes a lot of time.'*
>
> Regional textiles exporter

customs clearance. Occasionally, just one single agent seems to be in charge, and this reportedly 'incites bad behaviour' by the companies and officials, such as the payment of bribes to reduce waiting times.

Furthermore, inspection personnel often appear to be insufficiently trained on the different requirements they must deal with, including rules of origin, the different types of taxes and charges, customs valuation, product classification

> *'The customs authority re-evaluates the commercial invoice value. Usually the valuated customs value of the imported goods is 50% higher than the original value.'*
>
> Regional manufactured products exporter

and quality exigencies. This leads to misjudgements and unpredictable, inconsistent decisions, for example on the customs valuation of a shipment.

Product handling is another major concern. Many companies complain about products being damaged during inspections, caused at times by a lack of expertise on how a product is

> *'The partner country's customs authority requires a physical inspection of the products, which usually exposes them to damage. Glass products are fragile and require careful handling. Many times the products were smashed in the discharge port, either while unloading or during inspection.'*
>
> Regional glassware exporter

to be handled, or by carelessness. This is reported both for pre-shipment inspections on the exporter's side of the border and for customs clearance in the destination country. The impact of mishandling is more severe when there is a requirement for '100% inspections'. Such inspections usually oblige exporters to unload all pieces from a container, which increases the likelihood of damage.

PREDICTABILITY AND TRANSPARENCY

Access to information is a cross-cutting issue that also causes problems with customs clearance and border controls. Many exporters, especially novices, are ill-informed about what documentation to bring or where to obtain it. Some exporters can be blamed for being unprepared. However, inadequately publicized or frequently changing procedures can hinder adequate preparation.

Lack of transparency affects companies, but it ultimately boomerangs back to the customs authority itself when personnel are confronted with unprepared companies that cause bottlenecks and delays. As mentioned previously in relation to SPS and TBT measures, inadequate publication and dissemination of requirements can also create confusion among the officials themselves, while reducing the possibility for exporters to verify or appeal ambiguous regulations and decisions.

> *'At the last customs point before entering the partner country, officials ask to reinspect the whole shipment – knowing it has already been inspected at another customs point.*
>
> *'The process causes delays of up to two–three days and may damage the goods if they need refrigeration.'*

Regional food products exporter

COORDINATION BETWEEN AGENCIES

Lack of coordination between the many agencies or places involved in controlling shipments, and between countries, can lead to unnecessary delays and duplication of inspections.

First, technical and non-technical inspections, which are usually carried out by different entities, may have different service hours and availabilities or may not cooperate enough to ensure smooth handling and coordination, for example in transmitting documents.

> *'We constantly face exaggerated inspections on products that we have exported for many years. Each single batch is repeatedly controlled.'*

Regional clothing exporter

Second, companies must generally pass through several customs points, especially when transiting through third countries. Often the same procedures are repeated over and over again.

Finally, destination countries often do not trust the controls carried out in the exporting country and insist on repeating them. A number of Arab countries require inspections to be conducted by private companies such as SGS or Bureau Veritas, instead of by public authorities, which adds considerably to the cost of exporting.

Redundancies in the procedure inflate the time needed to export and compromise timely shipping, which is imperative – particularly for perishable goods.

> *'The partner country's customs authority requires pre-shipment inspection by SGS or Bureau Veritas, which is usually expensive and doesn't add any value.'*

Regional cooking appliances exporter

LENGTH AND COSTS OF CUSTOMS CLEARANCE

The above-mentioned impediments to efficient customs clearance make the customs experience cumbersome for most surveyed companies and explain the frequency with which customs authorities both at home and abroad mention procedural obstacles (table 2). The clearance procedure is perceived as:

- **Lengthy**, with 'unnecessary' delays in the completion of documentation, ranging from a few days to several weeks;
- **Bureaucratic and disorganized**, involving a lot of paperwork and different administrative windows;
- **Costly**, because (of a combination) of:
  - Inspection charges of more than US$ 200 per shipment, especially when exporters and importers are obliged to use the services of private companies;
  - The request for or payment of bribes (e.g. US$ 85 per truck) in order to circumvent long delays or product damage;
  - Different fees and charges (such as high merchandise handling fees), which are not always known in advance.

All of these issues contribute to the perception of clearance procedures as unpredictable.

CHAPTER 6

CONCLUSIONS AND RECOMMENDATIONS

CONCLUSIONS AND RECOMMENDATIONS

Key messages to boost intra-Arab trade

- Market access begins at home. The upside of home-made problems is that they can be solved more easily than those outside a country's or region's jurisdiction. The survey findings underscore the fact that there is wide scope for action on tackling the before-the-border problems which businesses face with behind-the-border measures.

- There is a need to make agreements work and possibly to do more work on existing agreements, particularly GAFTA. The survey findings support the conventional wisdom that having policies, laws and agreements is one thing, but effectively implementing them is another. Making existing agreements work – including GAFTA, mutual recognition agreements, the revised Kyoto Convention and the more recent Trade Facilitation Agreement[7] – can contribute significantly to trade facilitation and would eliminate many of the concerns raised by the businesses surveyed.

- Transparency is pivotal to facilitating Arab trade. Procedures may be complicated and lengthy for good reasons, but there is no good reason for them to be unclear and non-transparent. Providing information contributes to more efficient procedures and reduced trade costs, by making cross-border business transactions more predictable in terms of time and cost.

The data from the ITC NTM Surveys of exporters and importers in Egypt, Morocco, the State of Palestine and Tunisia show that private-sector concerns about NTMs are manifold and not limited to the strictness of the regulations themselves.

Most obstacles to intraregional trade reported in the surveys are procedural in nature. As such, they can be tackled pragmatically by facilitating trade rather than changing the underlying trade rules.

THE HIGH-LEVEL ROUNDTABLE ON NTMS

The NTM Survey findings served as input to the discussion at the 2014 Tunis regional roundtable on NTMs. Three thematic sessions addressed quality and conformity requirements; rules of origin and other trade-related measures; and customs clearance and border controls, and formulated recommendations.

The rest of this chapter synthesizes and elaborates on the roundtable's recommendations. Where appropriate, it places each issue in context and provides the rationale for the recommendations.

TRANSPARENCY – A CROSS-CUTTING ISSUE

Transparency is pivotal to facilitating intraregional and international trade and to mitigating the negative impact of NTMs.[8] It is a cross-cutting issue in all the surveys. The recommendations focus on the importance of disseminating information and on the capacity-building needed for information and data collection.

PROCEDURES, RESPONSE TIMES AND FEES

The NTM Survey findings point to the need for improving both the transparency of official procedures and the response times and fees for all institutions involved in the export and import process. This will render trading more

---

7   Available from http://www.wto.org/english/tratop_e/tradfa_e/tradfa_e.htm. Accessed 7 September 2015.

8   See the OECD research work, such as Moïsé, E. (2011), *Transparency Mechanisms and Non-Tariff Measures: Case Studies*, OECD Trade Policy Papers, No. 111, OECD Publishing, available from http://dx.doi.org/10.1787/5kgf0rzzwfq3-en; or Fliess, B. (2014), *Transparency of Export Restrictions: A Checklist Promoting Good Practice*, OECD Trade Policy Papers, No. 164, OECD Publishing, available from http://dx.doi.org/10.1787/5jz417hqk38q-en.

predictable in terms of time and cost. Transparency in these areas reduces incentives for bribes, which are often exchanged because official fees are opaque or because procedures such as customs clearance and certification are overly lengthy and unpredictable.

Publish and update official deadlines and response times

Official handling deadlines and response times for the various procedures (for example 'within five working days'), as well as the associated fees, should be published, regularly updated and actively disseminated. This would allow Arab States to comply with the requirements under art.1 and art.6, para. 1.2, of the WTO Trade Facilitation Agreement.

Institutions should make use of all types of methods and technologies for disseminating information and interacting with clients, such as web-based portals, brochures, helpdesks and helplines, and ensure regular opening days for agencies and institutions.

Adopt a tracking system

Institutions should adopt a tracking system for requests, complaints and other correspondence. This would allow companies to follow the handling of their requests and shed light on what many companies perceive as a 'black box' of administrative procedures. Such a tracking system would also provide valuable statistics for institutions, enabling them to better monitor the quality and speed of handling requests and inquiries and to take corrective action where needed.

Tracking systems should be accompanied by enquiry mechanisms to enable companies to follow up on requests and to ask for an official response when officially published deadlines are not respected.

These recommendations are aimed at increasing the accountability of institutions and their employees and decreasing the frequency of the 'arbitrary behaviour' attributed to officials.

ADDRESSING THE INFORMATION GAP

Exporters often find it easier to obtain information about third markets, for example the European Union, than about regional export destinations. This is a serious impediment to regional integration.

Establish a regional trade information portal

A comprehensive regional trade information portal should be established on market access conditions, regulations and related procedures in Arab States, following the model of portals in other regions, such as the EU Export Helpdesk.

The recent ITC-led EuroMed Trade and Investment Facilitation Mechanism should be extended in scope geographically beyond the Mediterranean Arab States.[9] Its data coverage should go beyond official regulations on exports and imports to include information on related procedures and existing dispute settlement mechanisms. Providing this information would enhance the visibility of changes in legislation for policymakers and businesses in partner countries within and beyond the region. This would facilitate timely notification and make it possible to react to changes in partner countries' legislations.

Establish a network for information exchange and coordination

The portal should contain the contact details of national enquiry points in all Arab States in order to give exporters and importers access to more information or to seek clarifications. These enquiry points should be interlinked at the regional level to establish a network for information exchange and coordination. (See the recommendations below on mechanisms to facilitate the implementation of existing agreements.)

Create regional export guides

In preparing the portal, regional export guides should be drafted to address the most critical information gaps identified by the NTM Survey findings, including:

- An Arab States guide to labelling and traceability requirements.
- A mapping of applied quality standards and related processes in Arab States. The information collected for the forthcoming region-specific version of the ITC *Export Quality Management: A Guide for Small and Medium-Sized Exporters*[10] could be a valuable starting point for this mapping.
- An Arab States guide to customs procedures, which, in addition to providing useful information for businesses, would allow Arab States to anticipate the implementation of the corresponding requirements under the Trade Facilitation Agreement.

---

9   For more information on the mechanism, see http://www.intracen.org/euromed/ (accessed 7 September 2015).

10   A generic version of the guide is available in English and Arabic: ITC (2011), *Export Quality Management: A Guide for Small and Medium-Sized Exporters*, Second Edition, available from http://www.intracen.org/export-quality-management-a-guide-for-small-and-medium-sized-exporters-second-ed/ (English version; accessed 7 September 2015) and from http://www.intracen.org/publication/Export-Quality-Management-A-Guide-for-Small-and-Medium-Sized-Exporters-arabic/ (Arabic version; accessed 7 September 2015).

The regional export guides should contain information on applied regulations and procedures in Arab States. They should highlight similarities and – potentially even more important – differences among countries.

Increase opportunities for regional business matchmaking

To close the significant information gap on business opportunities in regional markets, trade and investment promotion organizations and TISIs should increase opportunities for regional business matchmaking. This could be done by:

- Organizing regional trade fairs;
- Creating new distribution channels, such as virtual marketplaces;[11]
- Publishing comprehensive, publicly available and easily accessible business directories, such as the company-level information displayed in the ITC Trade Map, which highlights the contact details of companies exporting or importing for a given product and country, so as to facilitate sourcing and selling.

AWARENESS-RAISING, CAPACITY-BUILDING AND ADVISORY SERVICES

In parallel with 'passive' information dissemination through publications and an enquiry-based information mechanism, institutions in Arab States, supported by the relevant ministries and in collaboration with TISIs, should step up their active outreach through awareness-raising campaigns and capacity-building.

Offer training on international trade agreements

Ongoing, in-depth training sessions should be offered to the private and public sector on international trade agreements, including:

- The WTO agreements on TBTs and on the application of SPS measures to quality-related issues;
- The revised Kyoto Convention and the Trade Facilitation Agreement, for customs-related matters;
- GAFTA and bilateral trade agreements, for trade rules and rules of origin.

Enhance the advisory services offer of trade and investment support institutions

TISIs should enhance their advisory services offer, particularly for SMEs, including those located in remote regions. Public agencies such as standards institutes and customs authorities should hold regular training sessions on product certification and customs clearance procedures.

SMEs should be actively informed and trained on customs procedures, rules of origin, product valuation practices and regulatory surveillance for exporters as a first step towards overcoming procedural obstacles related to these requirements.

Capacity-building initiatives should involve innovative delivery methods, such as e-learning.

QUALITY AND CONFORMITY ASSESSMENT REQUIREMENTS

The recommendations on quality and conformity requirements focus on: (1) regional standardization and conformity assessment; (2) harmonizing standards; (3) conformity assessment procedures; (4) mutual recognition; (5) support to enterprises on complying with technical measures; and (6) the technical regulatory framework.

Identify priority sectors and products

To ensure feasibility and high impact, the roundtable participants recommended identifying priority sectors and products on the basis of their potential to drive regional integration, and subsequently concentrating standard-setting efforts and improvements in the conformity assessment infrastructure on those products and sectors.

REGIONAL STANDARDIZATION AND CONFORMITY ASSESSMENT

Existing regional standardization and conformity assessment strategies, including their achievements and implementation, should be reviewed to identify outstanding gaps. The survey findings confirm the need for supporting the relevant activities of the United Nations Industrial Development Organization (UNIDO), which are aimed at updating and revising the regional standardization strategy of the Arab Industrial Development and Mining Organization.

Cooperate on the international standard-setting process

Arab States should work together to coordinate regional negotiating positions effectively on the international standard-setting process.

---

11   A joint ITC/World Bank project is aimed at coaching SMEs in Jordan, Morocco and Tunisia to become more active and to benefit from business opportunities offered by international virtual marketplaces. The project is funded by the Transition Fund, established by the Deauville Partnership with Arab Countries in Transition.

HARMONIZING STANDARDS AND TECHNICAL REQUIREMENTS

The implementation of Arab regional standards, and the regional standard-setting mechanism, should be reviewed to identify concrete measures for improvements and to make the mechanism more inclusive. Priority should be given to:

- Creating an inventory of regional standards and analysing their legal status and relevance both within the region and vis-à-vis international standards;
- Helping national standards bodies to participate in the regional standard-setting process, including in national technical committees, and promoting private-sector participation in the process;
- Creating or increasing support to national and regional sector-specific trade associations, particularly for priority sectors of intraregional trade.

Harmonize labelling requirements

Given the high incidence of private-sector concerns about labelling, special attention should be paid to harmonizing labelling requirements. A standardized 'Arab label' in Arabic, French and English could reduce the cost of customizing labels and facilitate intraregional trade. This could be complemented with and in the immediate term replaced by a regularly updated and detailed Arab States guide mapping national differences in labelling requirements for food and non-food products. This guide should be publicly available and widely disseminated.

CONFORMITY ASSESSMENT

The following actions should be undertaken with respect to conformity assessment:

- Examine conformity assessment procedures, including testing, certification and inspection procedures at national level, and develop a roadmap for their harmonization within the region based on best practices.
- Map the region's testing needs and private and public capacities for priority sectors. Assess the business model and financial sustainability of laboratories as well as their accessibility from abroad.
- Designate reference laboratories for the Arab region that could cater to regional testing needs. Upgrade technical infrastructure where needed and support the accreditation of these laboratories. Improve their accessibility from abroad.
- Strengthen the capacity of priority inspection and certification bodies at national level to comply with international requirements, working towards accreditation when necessary.

MUTUAL RECOGNITION

The NTM Survey findings point to the need to ensure effective mutual recognition of test results and certification in order to avoid costly duplication. Designating accredited reference laboratories could contribute in the long term. However, complementary solutions need to be found for the products and sectors that contribute to intraregional trade but which are not considered priority products or sectors.

Mutual recognition agreements and memoranda for conformity assessment should be reviewed to identify obstacles to their effective implementation, and support must be provided to countries and institutions to eliminate them.

Where mutual recognition agreements do not exist, Arab States should work towards establishing them. Another solution would be to identify alternative ways to simplify cross-border acceptance of conformity assessments, such as increased harmonization of standards.

COMPLIANCE WITH TECHNICAL REQUIREMENTS

Remedying the inability of many companies to comply with technical requirements depends on enhancing the capacity of TISIs in training and advisory services. Enterprises in the identified priority sectors for intraregional trade should receive targeted support to improve their compliance.

Compliance also has financial implications, and high costs and fees are a de facto impediment to SME exports. One solution would be to establish a mechanism whereby the first test would be free for SMEs that passed it successfully. This could incentivize quality production and motivate SMEs to seek information about technical requirements before undertaking product tests and certification. Subsequent tests could be financed through an export support loan to cover the initial investment in testing, which would be repaid once the tested and certified product was sold. This would lower the testing and certification threshold for first-time exports of SMEs.

The need for affordable tests and certification should always be evaluated in conjunction with the need for laboratories and certification-issuing bodies to be profitable or to break even. Sustainable financial mechanisms for those bearing the costs should be accompanied by reviewing the cost and revenue structure of those writing the bills.

Create sustainable financial mechanisms

Arab States should create sustainable financial mechanisms, particularly for SMEs, to:

- Enable them to upgrade production processes, traceability and product quality in line with international requirements;
- Make testing and certification affordable.

Improve the availability and accessibility of training on quality requirements

Arab States should improve the availability of training on quality requirements and its accessibility for smaller enterprises and those located in remote regions, as follows:

- National standards bodies and certification agencies should review and develop their training activities to ensure effective outreach, particularly to SMEs. Training could be offered in collaboration with trade promotion organizations and private-sector associations.

- National standards bodies or relevant ministries should institutionalize regular training sessions provided by international experts and standards bodies, such as the International Organization for Standardization.

- A 'twinning programme' could be established to enable the standards body of one Arab State to train companies in another on its national quality requirements. For example, the more advanced Arab States and those with more stringent quality requirements, such as the countries in the Gulf region, could train companies in the region's less advanced countries. Priority could be given to sectors and products that are import priorities for the destination countries, which would ensure the feasibility of a twinning programme.

- Direct capacity-building on specific quality requirements from buyers in the region could be delivered to existing or potential exporters of the requested products. This approach has worked in selected sectors and products elsewhere, and could be replicated in Arab States to establish regional value chains and boost intraregional trade.

TECHNICAL REGULATORY FRAMEWORK

- **Raise awareness and promote effective implementation of good regulatory practices**, for example, for the required frequency of renewal of certifications and authorizations. National legislation on SPS and TBTs, together with related conformity assessment procedures, should be assessed in the light of the principles put forward in WTO agreements, which stipulate that measures shall not be more trade-restrictive than necessary to fulfil a legitimate objective, such as the appropriate level of SPS protection. Where they already exist, less trade-restrictive measures that do not compromise the level of legitimate protection should be adopted.

- **Promote best practices of market surveillance at national level and ensure coordination at regional level.**

- **Create a coordination mechanism among national regulatory institutions, inspection bodies and TISIs.**

ADDRESSING TRADE-RELATED MEASURES

Recommendations on trade-related measures are the most difficult to formulate, as their viability depends on the degree of political priority that Arab States place on regional trade integration. According to a 2014 United Nations report on Arab integration,[12] the region's recent history is filled with initiatives and ambitious plans for greater economic integration, with the earliest regional agreements dating back to the 1950s. However, the potential benefits of these initiatives were often undermined by poor implementation.

The United Nations report notes that so far, 'the Arab countries have missed many of the opportunities and benefits associated with economic integration and the creation of a regional market'.[13] Past experience demonstrates that Arab States find it challenging to reconcile the goal of greater intraregional trade integration with other political considerations, including, but not limited to, further developing national production and looking towards third markets outside the region.

Against this background, it is more practical to work primarily at the level of procedural obstacles and the trade support infrastructure than to focus on the trade rules and agreements. This approach addresses the less contentious issue of creating a business environment conducive to trade in general, whether intraregional or beyond, regardless of whether there is momentum for increased political backing of regional integration efforts.

The recommendations below therefore start by addressing procedural obstacles and the trade support infrastructure before turning to mechanisms to facilitate the implementation of existing rules, legislation and agreements and, finally, to the trade rules and agreements themselves. The recommendations complement those on increasing transparency, which concern access to information on trade rules and procedures.

PROCEDURAL OBSTACLES AND THE TRADE SUPPORT INFRASTRUCTURE

Most procedural obstacles reported by the surveyed exporters and importers concern administrative inefficiencies in the home State. Streamlining procedures, reducing bureaucracy and alleviating administrative burdens will contribute substantially to reducing those obstacles and enhancing trade facilitation.

---

12   United Nations Economic and Social Commission for Western Asia (2014). *Arab Integration – A 21st Century Development Imperative*. Beirut, February 2014. Available online in Arabic, English and French from http://www.escwa.un.org/information/pubaction.asp?PubID=1550 (accessed 7 September 2015).

13   *Ibid.*, 53.

Invest in people and trade support infrastructure

The NTM Survey findings show that investment in people is crucial. Sufficient and well-trained staff in the public institutions involved in the export and import process, including ministries, other certification-issuing agencies and the customs authority, together with avoiding frequent staff turnover, will help reduce delays in administrative procedures.

Administrative burdens can be further alleviated through investment in infrastructure, and particularly in systems for the electronic submission of documents and storage of information so as to eliminate the need to duplicate and resubmit documents that are still valid. For example, clear deadlines for issuing certificates of origin should be established and respected. Governments should revisit the requirement for companies to reapply for certificates of origin for each shipment. Instead of examining each application with the same scrutiny, ministries should implement simplified fast-track procedures when the same products are repeatedly exported by the same company within a reasonably short period of time.

Electronic systems can also enhance the interconnectedness among different agencies, including laboratories, certification bodies, ministries, the customs authority of the exporting State and, ideally, the customs authority of the importing Arab State. Test results or certificates of origin can be transmitted automatically by the issuing body to other administrations, which will expedite the export process, especially when many different administrative windows are involved. Electronic systems could also reduce the risk of forgery, which is sometimes the reason for the detailed and time-consuming examination of corporate documents.

Institutionalize advance ruling

In order to reduce uncertainties among enterprises and customs officials about the applicable rules of origin and the recognition of related certificates during the import process, it is indispensable to institutionalize advance ruling on product origin. The provisions of the Trade Facilitation Agreement must be implemented, whether or not a country is a WTO Member. This is also reflected in the recommendations on customs procedures.

Institutionalize ongoing public-private dialogue

As formalized in the Trade Facilitation Agreement, Arab States should institutionalize national trade facilitation committees or other forms of ongoing public-private dialogue. For these committees to be effective and of added value, they should be inclusive and extend to representatives of the customs authority, the private sector (from both the export and import side) and other stakeholders critical to trade, such as standards organizations and ministries of health, agriculture and trade.

National trade facilitation committees enable information on existing or envisaged rules and their application to be channelled from the public to the private sector. Such committees also provide a platform for the private sector to identify inefficiencies, highlight other concerns and identify solutions to existing problems.

Strengthen trade and investment support institutions

Strengthening trade support infrastructure involves acknowledging the pivotal role of TISIs in providing advisory services to enterprises. An effective network of such institutions with adequate outreach to small enterprises and remote regions can be an important link in the trade facilitation chain.

Managerial, operational and service delivery performance of TISIs should be strengthened to enable them more effectively to meet their clients' needs. The institutions must be in a position to understand market trends and the institutional landscape so as to better coordinate the delivery of their services, which includes providing information and advice about NTMs.

Key TISIs from the Arab region should have access to dedicated platforms where they can interact and address the issues hindering intraregional trade. This will enhance their capacity to lobby for improving domestic business environments. TISIs should be strengthened to enable them to organize targeted events, such as buyer-seller meetings, which facilitate business transactions and strategic partnerships between enterprises within the region.

Address inefficiencies in the wider business environment

In the longer term, Arab States will need to address serious inefficiencies in the wider business environment, notably with regard to SME access to trade finance and other trade-related services, as well as the inefficiency of transport infrastructure and logistics. With respect to trade finance, Arab States should review whether and how SMEs in their countries take advantage of the Arab Trade Financing Programme. They should determine how to improve the programme's outreach and its accessibility for SMEs and first-time exporters.

FACILITATING IMPLEMENTATION OF EXISTING AGREEMENTS

The NTM Survey findings, national stakeholder meetings in the surveyed economies and the Tunis roundtable all point to the Arab States' lack of well-functioning mechanisms at national and regional level for monitoring the implementation of agreements, particularly the GAFTA Agreement, and for identifying and resolving implementation problems.

Create a trade obstacles alert

Arab States should establish enquiry points or helpdesks for the private sector at the national level to respond to questions and complaints about obstacles to intraregional trade. The designated focal points for GAFTA and the Agadir Agreement should be activated or strengthened. The enquiry points should be part of a wider problem-solving network comprising contact points in the various trade-related agencies, passing on private-sector concerns and, where possible, taking action – particularly in the case of procedural obstacles.

If well designed, this trade obstacles alert mechanism could considerably improve monitoring and reporting on the effective implementation of existing agreements as well as effectively reducing procedural obstacles to their application.[14]

Regular, comprehensive regional studies, for example on the current status of application of rules of origin (de jure vs. de facto), could be an important complement to the complaints-based mechanism.

Implement interlinked focal points at regional level

In order to close implementation gaps, focal points should be interlinked at the regional level and should interact regularly, with the ability to submit questions and concerns and jointly identify solutions. Regular information exchange at the technical level among these focal points is crucial to compiling information about systematic implementation problems. It would help to distinguish between procedural issues that can be addressed at the technical level and those requiring more substantive decisions at higher political levels through regional summits or negotiations. (See the recommendations on regional institutional structures, below.)

Develop capacity to use existing trade agreements

In parallel with and beyond GAFTA, the capacity of Arab States to use the mechanisms offered by the various bilateral, regional and multilateral agreements must be developed. Dispute resolution mechanisms are one example. The less developed Arab States should be enabled to take advantage of the available assistance and mechanisms, for example through WTO, for challenging quantity control or anti-dumping measures.

Clarify and harmonize rules of origin

With respect to the trade rules themselves, an agreement on the rules of origin applicable under GAFTA must be reached if regional trade integration is to work. Rules of origin that are not clearly defined or agreed among member States render preferential trade impracticable for the specific products. This undermines the objectives of the GAFTA Agreement, which focuses on tariff elimination and preferential trade as a basis for greater regional integration.

It is necessary to clarify which rules of origin (if any) take precedence, and which certificates of origin are accepted at border stations in case of overlapping agreements with differing rules and related certificates.

Arab States should work towards harmonizing rules of origin across the region, including through an agreement on cumulation of origin. Procedures for issuing certificates of origin should be standardized.

Work together at regional level

Arab States should carefully review the different GAFTA measures that limit preferential trade, including negative lists, quantitative restrictions and burdensome import licensing schemes. Governments should evaluate the effectiveness and efficiency of these measures in terms of their own objectives, such as protecting national industries and employment in certain sectors. Where such measures exist, governments should implement less trade-distorting alternatives to achieve their objectives.

Arab States should work at the regional level on closing loopholes in GAFTA and should build an institutional structure that enables formulating, implementing and better monitoring of joint policies. Also needed are improved regional coordination of trade policies, better technical cooperation on harmonizing rules and procedures, and an effective dispute settlement mechanism. The role of the Arab Economic and Social Council should be reviewed and GAFTA-specific bodies established.

GAFTA-specific bodies will be indispensable if GAFTA member States pursue the goal of an Arab customs union and an Arab common market, as called for by successive Arab Economic and Social Development Summits in 2009, 2011 and 2013. A customs union will require comprehensive adaptation of the arrangements under trade agreements of Arab States with third countries so as to ensure coherence among the different commitments.

Provide special assistance to least developed Arab States

Tunis roundtable participants recognized the various levels of development across the Arab region and the need for special technical and financial assistance for its least developed members. They agreed on the need to examine the feasibility of an assistance programme to enable the more advanced Arab States to help the less advanced

---

14   This type of national alert system and associated problem-solving network is being piloted in Côte d'Ivoire and Mauritius. A regional initiative exists for member States of the East African Community, the Common Market for Eastern and Southern Africa and the Southern African Development Community.

develop their capacities in the areas of trade rules, customs clearance and trade infrastructure.

Special assistance could be delivered by a reimbursement mechanism to compensate for losses in earnings from tariffs and other fees.

CUSTOMS CLEARANCE AND BORDER CONTROLS

Arab States' customs authorities are the most important agencies on the path to regional trade integration and to a possible Arab customs union. Chapter 5 of this publication noted that the fundamental challenge for these institutions is to reconcile the mandate of revenue collection and product quality and safety control with the need to ensure a smooth export and import process. Arab States should apply the provisions set forth in the revised Kyoto Convention on the Simplification and Harmonization of Customs Procedures.

The NTM Survey findings highlight the potential and the need for significant rationalization of formalities at border crossings. Efficient risk management, paperless clearance, and benchmarking against and learning from success stories of other countries, particularly developing countries, are central to this endeavour. Roundtable participants stressed the need for diagnostics and comparative studies to identify best practices and determine the most effective ways of exchanging experiences among GAFTA members.

The following recommendations on customs clearance and border controls focus on: (1) legislation governing customs clearance and border controls; (2) customs procedures and infrastructure; (3) information and communication technologies (ICTs); (4) partnerships and information exchange; and (5) human resources.

Review customs legislation

Arab countries should review their customs legislation to determine conformity with their commitments under bilateral, regional and multilateral agreements and to coordinate among the various national entities.

Improve customs procedures and infrastructure

Arab States should strengthen risk analysis mechanisms to implement efficient risk management, thereby avoiding '100% inspections'.

Regular updates of requirements and procedures are necessary to reflect the reality of trade and border inspection needs in a constantly changing and modernizing world. An appropriate transitional system for implementing new legislation should be established, including:

- Provisions on due notice;
- Transparency – easy accessibility and wide dissemination of enacted changes;
- Clear guidelines on dealing with goods shipped before the application of a new rule but reaching the border thereafter;
- Facilitated interaction between economic operators and the customs authority through helplines and helpdesks.

Advance ruling, and filing and processing of documents, should be institutionalized where feasible.

Arab States should streamline customs clearance of goods in transit and perishable goods, for example through separate infrastructure or simplified procedures in line with international standards and agreements. (See arts. 9 and 10 of the Trade Facilitation Agreement.)

The necessary infrastructure for storage and customs clearance must be provided and regularly upgraded.

Arab States should institutionalize joint border controls to limit the number of inspections carried out and the time needed to cross a border.

Apply information and communication technologies to customs procedures

Customs administrations should be equipped with the latest technologies to increase efficiency. They should:

- Regularly update customs clearance systems based on the latest technologies;
- Adopt modern detection and surveillance technologies, including X-ray detectors;
- Use satellite systems and electronic tracking to monitor cross-border movements of goods;
- Institutionalize the acceptance of electronic copies of required documentation ('paperless clearance');
- Ensure electronic interconnectedness among institutions;
- Establish a single window for customs clearance;
- Based on national single windows, work towards a regional single window.

Tunis roundtable participants emphasized the importance of support from donors and specialized organizations to help Arab States acquire the necessary equipment to establish one-stop shops and adopt modern technologies for surveillance and information exchange.

Strengthen partnerships and information exchange

Partnerships and information exchange must be strengthened, both between the customs authorities of Arab States and between those of Arab States and third countries. Arab States should also:

- Create partnerships between customs administrations and the business community and between customs administrations of Arab States and international organizations and donors.
- Establish twinning programmes between customs administrations and their counterparts in the rest of the world, especially developing-country pioneers in modern border clearance systems, to learn from best practices.
- Organize field visits of customs officials to customs administrations, particularly in other Arab countries, to benefit from the experience of the more advanced countries in the region.
- Conclude or activate mutual administrative cooperation and information exchange agreements to combat fraud.

Strengthen human resources

Human resources at customs authorities and border stations should be strengthened to reduce the incidence of procedural obstacles.

Increase staff and institutionalize training

The number of staff should be increased where border clearance is inefficient due to insufficient human resources. Customs officials' capacities in the various customs disciplines should be enhanced through ongoing training on modern techniques, efficient risk management and the application of international conventions.

Customs authorities in Arab States should review or develop the training activities available to their staff and institutionalize ongoing training provided by national or international experts, for example in cooperation with the World Customs Organization or customs authorities from other Arab States and third countries.

Initiate a change in culture

Roundtable participants called for a general change in culture, whereby customs authorities would consider themselves a 'welcome point'. Customs officials are ambassadors at the border, representing their country and creating first impressions for visitors. They should be aware and proud of the important role they play in national well-being, security, economic development and regional integration. This should be reflected in their attitude on the job and in the recognition they receive.

ANNEXES

DATA SOURCES, REFERENCES AND FURTHER READING

DATA SOURCES, REFERENCES AND FURTHER READING

PUBLICLY AVAILABLE DATA SOURCES

ITC Market Analysis Tools, available from www.intracen.org/marketanalysis:

- Market Access Map (tariffs and market requirements)
- Trade Map (trade statistics)
- Standards Map (voluntary standards)
- Investment Map (foreign direct investment data)

NTM Survey data:

- http://ntmsurvey.intracen.org

INTERNAL ITC DATABASES

- NTM Survey database for cross-country data collected through the ITC business surveys on NTMs, ITC Market Analysis and Research section
- Trade agreements monitoring database, ITC Market Analysis and Research section

REFERENCES AND FURTHER READING

Fliess, B. (2014). *Transparency of Export Restrictions: A Checklist Promoting Good Practice*. OECD Trade Policy Papers, No. 164, OECD Publishing. Available from http://dx.doi.org/10.1787/5jz417hqk38q-en. Accessed 7 September 2015.

International Trade Centre (2011). *Export Quality Management: A Guide for Small and Medium-Sized Exporters*. Second Edition. Available from http://www.intracen.org/export-quality-management-a-guide-for-small-and-medium-sized-exporters-second-ed/. Accessed 7 September 2015.

Moïsé, E. (2011). *Transparency Mechanisms and Non-Tariff Measures: Case Studies*. OECD Trade Policy Papers, No. 111, OECD Publishing. Available from http://dx.doi.org/10.1787/5kgf0rzzwfq3-en. Accessed 7 September 2015.

United Nations Economic and Social Commission for Western Asia (2014). *Arab Integration – A 21st Century Development Imperative*. Beirut, United Nations Publishing. Available online in Arabic, English and French from http://www.escwa.un.org/information/pubaction.asp?PubID=1550. Accessed 7 September 2015.

World Bank (2012). *From political to economic awakening in the Arab World: the path of economic integration - a Deauville partnership report on trade and foreign direct investment: overview report. MENA development report*. Washington, D.C.: World Bank. Available from http://documents.worldbank.org/curated/en/2012/05/16720713/political-economic-awakening-arab-world-path-economic-integration-deauville-partnership-report-trade-foreign-direct-investment-overview-report. Accessed 1 October 2015.

SELECTED INTERNATIONAL AGREEMENTS

Agreement on the Application of Sanitary and Phytosanitary Measures (SPS Agreement). Available from https://www.wto.org/english/tratop_e/sps_e/spsagr_e.htm. Accessed 1 October 2015.

Agreement on Technical Barriers to Trade (TBT Agreement). Available from https://www.wto.org/english/docs_e/legal_e/17-tbt_e.htm. Accessed 1 October 2015.

Revised Kyoto Convention on the Simplification and Harmonization of Customs Procedures. Available from http://www.wcoomd.org/en/topics/facilitation/instrument-and-tools/conventions/pf_revised_kyoto_conv/kyoto_new.aspx. Accessed 9 October 2015.

Trade Facilitation Agreement. Available from http://www.wto.org/english/tratop_e/tradfa_e/tradfa_e.htm. Accessed 7 September 2015.

THE ITC PUBLICATION SERIES ON NON-TARIFF MEASURES

COUNTRY REPORTS

Sri Lanka: Company perspectives (English, 2011)
Burkina Faso: Company perspectives (French, 2011)
Morocco: Company perspectives (French, 2012)
Peru: Company perspectives (English, 2012; Spanish, 2013)
Malawi: Company perspectives (English, 2013)
Trinidad and Tobago: Company perspectives (English, 2013)
Uruguay: Company perspectives (Spanish, 2013)
Jamaica: Company perspectives (English, 2013)
Madagascar: Company perspectives (French, 2013)
Paraguay: Company perspectives (Spanish, 2013)
Mauritius: Company perspectives (English, 2014)
Rwanda: Company perspectives (English, 2014)
Kenya: Company perspectives (English, 2014)
Senegal: Company perspectives (French, 2014)
Côte d'Ivoire: Company perspectives (French, 2014)
Cambodia: Company perspectives (English, 2014)
Tunisia: Company perspectives (French, 2014)
Kazakhstan: Company perspectives (English, Russian. 2014)
State of Palestine: Company perspectives (English, 2015)
Guinea: Company perspectives (French, 2015)

FORTHCOMING

Egypt: Company perspectives (English)
Indonesia: Company perspectives (English)
Thailand: Company perspectives (English)
Colombia: Company perspectives (Spanish)
Bangladesh: Company perspectives (English)

RELATED PUBLICATIONS

NTMs and the fight against malaria: Obstacles to trade in anti-malarial commodities (English, 2011)

The invisible barriers to trade – How businesses experience non-tariff measures (English, 2015; French and Spanish forthcoming)

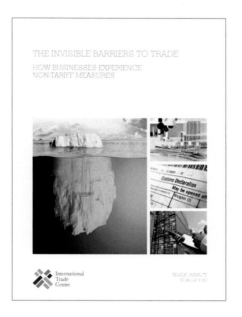